Azar 70-/75-

IMAGES OF AMERICAN INDIANS
ON FILM

GARLAND REFERENCE LIBRARY
OF SOCIAL SCIENCE
(VOL. 307)

IMAGES OF AMERICAN INDIANS ON FILM
An Annotated Bibliography

Gretchen M. Bataille
Charles L.P. Silet

GARLAND PUBLISHING INC. • NEW YORK & LONDON
1985

© 1985 Gretchen M. Bataille and Charles L.P. Silet
All rights reserved

Library of Congress Cataloging in Publication Data

Bataille, Gretchen M., 1944–
  Images of American Indians on film.

  (Garland reference library of social science ;
v. 307)
  Filmography: p.
  Includes index.
  1. Indians in motion pictures—Bibliography.
I. Silet, Charles, L. P. II. Title. III. Series.
Z5784.M9B388   1985   016.79143′09′093520397   84-48882
[PN1995.9.I48]
ISBN 0-8240-8737-2 (alk. paper)

Printed on acid-free, 250-year-life paper
Manufactured in the United States of America

This book is for
Adrienne Mueller
and
Peter Silet

CONTENTS

List of Illustrations	ix
Preface	xi
Acknowledgments	xv
Introduction	xvii
General Background	3
Articles and Books on American Indians in Films	19
Reviews of Individual Films	57
Illustrations	97
Listing of Sound Films Dealing with American Indians	117
Index	199

ILLUSTRATIONS

1. *The Squaw Man* (1918) — 97
2. *The Scarlet West* (1925) — 98
3. Jim Thorpe with Carl Lemmele — 99
4. *Buffalo Bill* (1944) — 100
5. *They Died with Their Boots On* (1941) — 100
6. *The Plainsman* (1936) — 101
7. *The Unconquered* (1947) — 101
8. *Northwest Passage* (1940) — 102
9. *Seminole* (1953) — 102
10. *Tonka* (1958) — 103
11. *Rio Grande* (1950) — 104
12. *Cheyenne Autumn* (1964) — 105
13. *Cheyenne Autumn* (1964) — 105
14. *A Man Called Horse* (1970) — 106
15. *The Way West* (1967) — 106
16. *McKenna's Gold* (1969) — 107
17. *Flap* (1970) — 108
18. *Little Big Man* (1970) — 109
19. *Little Big Man* (1970) — 109
20. *One Flew Over the Cuckoo's Nest* (1975) — 110
21. *Tell Them Willie Boy Is Here* (1969) — 110
22. *Billy Jack* (1972) — 111
23. *Jeremiah Johnson* (1972) — 111
24. *White Buffalo* (1977) — 112
25. *Broken Arrow* (1950) — 112
26. *When the Legends Die* (1972) — 113
27. *White Buffalo* (1977) — 114

Preface

In order to make this bibliography as useful as possible, we have provided the reader with an historical introduction, an appendix of information on individual films, and a comprehensive index as well as the bibliographic entries themselves. Our intent is to create a resource which will stimulate further research into how films treat minority cultures in general and American Indian cultures in particular.

The Introduction is designed to promote an understanding of the sources available to moviemakers for their depiction of the American Indian. We begin with the earliest contact between white Europeans and American Indians and discuss the evolution of the various images presented in non-film media, especially those generated by nineteenth-century popular culture which form the immediate link with the early movies. We also discuss the extension of those images in the history of the American film from its beginnings at the turn of the century to the present. Finally, the Introduction also includes a brief assessment of contemporary trends in depictions of American Indians in movies.

The Bibliography is divided into four separate sections. The first section contains books or essays which present broad general approaches to understanding American Indians as seen by the dominant white culture. Among such studies are Roy Harvey Pearce's SAVAGISM AND CIVILIZATION: A STUDY OF THE INDIAN AND THE AMERICAN MIND, Richard Slotkin's REGENERATION THROUGH VIOLENCE: THE MYTHOLOGY OF THE AMERICAN FRONTIER, 1600-1860, and Richard Drinnon's FACING WEST: THE METAPHYSICS OF INDIAN-HATING AND EMPIRE-BUILDING. Such works are useful because they provide an understanding of the intellectual as well as historical background of the movie images. This category is highly selective, but we have tried to include a sampling of the various types of studies and those which would broaden the reader's knowledge of popular attitudes about the American Indians.

The second section contains general studies on the Indian in film. These books and essays deal only with the treatment of American Indians on film. Most of the material in this section is comparative in nature, dealing with more than one historical period or film. The items cited provide a general overview of how American Indians have been treated in the movies during the past ninety years. The essays in this section often present contrasting points of view as they reflect changing attitudes toward Indians as well as the medium of film itself. A small number of essays actually exhibit racist attitudes which have for the most part vanished from the critical scholarship concerned with the treatment of American Indians on the screen. We have included such essays to help the reader understand the bias which was not only _in_ the movies but which also remained outside the films in the criticism.

The third section includes individual reviews and essays whose scope is a single film. Many of these items are reviews written for daily newspapers or weekly journals and contain the immediate reactions of the reviewer. Such criticism is extremely valuable insofar as it reflects a specific critical response, one which often mirrors popular taste more closely than do less spontaneous critical essays produced by writers who have more leisure to consider their subject. We have included reviews for major films dealing with American Indians which were published in those journals and newspapers which most affect informed public opinion.

The last section lists a selected number of important films which include American Indians as subjects. We have provided the date, running time, and color of the films as well as the director and the primary actors. This section was designed to supply the researcher with immediately accessible information for further study. We have chosen the films which are most likely to be available to the researcher either on television, from film society programs, or through one of the many film archives across the country. For a more comprehensive list of films, consult Ralph and Natasha Friar's THE ONLY GOOD INDIAN (108) and for documentaries, see Elizabeth Weatherford's NATIVE AMERICANS ON FILM AND VIDEO (186).

Finally, the index lists the film titles, major actors, directors, and other specific individuals connected with the films themselves. We hope that by so doing we can provide the reader with easy access to the materials we have compiled.

Acknowledgments

The authors would like to thank the following individuals and institutions for permission to reprint materials which originally appeared in their publications: Ronald Gottesman, editor, QUARTERLY REVIEW OF FILM STUDIES; Merritt Bailey, Director, Iowa State University Press; Charles C. Irby, Editor, NATIONAL ASSOCIATION FOR INTERDISCIPLINARY ETHNIC STUDIES NEWSLETTER; Michael T. Marsden and John G. Nachbar, editors, THE JOURNAL OF POPULAR FILM AND TELEVISION; Randall M. Miller, editor, THE KALEIDOSCOPIC LENS: ETHNIC IMAGES IN AMERICAN FILM; and the American Film Institute. We would like to acknowledge these individuals and organizations for giving us the opportunity to publish our research as it progressed. We also wish to thank the Museum of Modern Art and the Iowa State University Research Foundation for permission to use the photographs in this volume.

We owe an additional debt to the following persons who have provided us with support of varying kinds during the years this bibliography was being compiled: Donald Benson, former Chair, and Frank Haggard, Chair, Department of English, Iowa State University; Daniel J. Zaffarano, Vice President for Research and Dean of the Graduate School, Iowa State University; Donald Pady and the interlibrary loan staff of the University Library, Iowa State University; Stephan Storkel, Terry Grayson, and Phyllis Mann, who helped produce the final manuscript. Finally we have some personal debts to those who worked closely on the book. Terry Abbott, Carol Palmquist, and most particularly, Sheryl Kamps, who were needed for their typing and computing skills and their patience; Kay Silet, who supported yet one more joint project; Charles Irby, who offered advice and wise council; and Emily, Erin, Karin, Kris, Marc, and Scott, who gave us the main reason to do this project in the first place.

G.M.B.
C.L.P.S.

Introduction

The images of the American Indian which traditionally have been seen in motion pictures pre-date the invention of the motion picture camera by at least two hundred years. In fact they pre-date the discovery of America. The purpose of this introduction is to trace, in a brief fashion, the history of the misrepresentation of the American Indian which developed through the years since first contact was made between native peoples and white Europeans on the eastern shores of this continent. The misconceptions which whites hold about Indians are durable and derive from the earliest literature and graphic arts produced as a result of European expansion to the west. Although there have been minor alterations in those original images, for the most part the stereotypes created by the first pioneers still operate in our culture. When they began to depict American Indians, filmmakers merely accepted the existing popular images and transferred them onto film; they perpetuated a long and durable history of misrepresentation. As with other popular art forms of the twentieth century, the movie industry had a viable tradition on which to draw during its early developmental years. The sources of that tradition and the impact it had on the visual treatment of American Indian peoples is readily traceable.

I

When the Europeans came to the American continent they were faced with a dual problem: what to do with the wilderness and what to do with those who inhabited it. The first colonials wanted to subdue the new world and to bring order to what they perceived as chaos, to create a civilized society much like the one they had left in Europe. One of the impediments to this goal was the American Indian, and early colonists set about civilizing the "savage." Unfortunately, in doing so, the settlers exorcised their intense psychological and social anxieties by violent confrontation with the <u>dark forces of nature and humanity</u> of which "the Indian" became the focus.

The Puritans established a set of national attitudes and traditions which relied on the confrontation with the Indian to support their definition of the new settler who was to become the "American" or "New Adam." The initial impulses of the colonists, however finally disastrous, were at least well-intentioned. They wanted to bring American Indians into the emerging Euroamerican social order. But the American Indians were unwilling to accommodate the expectations of the Europeans. By the end of the 1770s the colonists had a new world vision in which the Indian played no part. The American Indian seemed bound inexorably to a primitive past, a primitive society, and a primitive environment, one which must make way for "civilization," and after the dawning of the Republic, the Indian became an unfortunate obstacle in the path of progress. The new society which white Americans built for themselves demanded the assurances of power and superiority--and the Indian became the point of comparison. The transition in mental attitudes from assimilation to annihilation was not an abrupt one, but by the beginning of the nineteenth century there was public recognition of both the failure in theory and in practice of the white attitude toward assimilation. Since the Indians would not conform to the way of life of the new society, nor be civilized, they had to be destroyed.[1]

An ambivalence toward the American Indian was reflected in the earliest accounts of life in the New World. In the journals of explorers such as Christopher Columbus and John Smith, then later in histories by government officials such as William Byrd and William Bradford, descriptions of the Indians depicted varying qualities of generosity, barbarity, or piety. During the seventeenth and eighteenth centuries, the captivity narratives

reinforced the existing Puritan explanation of the
Indians as subhuman or inspired by the devil. This
view of the Indian remained a powerful theme and,
although the hope of "civilizing" the Indian was
often expressed, ultimately civilization demanded
that the confrontation between Indian and white
result in Indian capitulation to white domination.
Individual Indians could be "good," but the group had
to be depicted as "bad" to justify the existing
exploitation by government and religious authorities.

Relying on contemporary documents and stories,
James Fenimore Cooper created both the noble and
ignoble savages as stock characters in American
literature. However, Cooper's The Leatherstocking
Tales were preceded by a number of other nineteenth-
century works that drew on the conventions of the
English historical romance of Walter Scott as well as
the savage prototypes created in earlier frontier
accounts. Robert Montgomery Bird's NICK OF THE WOODS
(1837) and William Gilmore Simms' THE YEMASSEE (1835)
reinforced existing attitudes. These works of
fiction were bolstered by the epic sweep of such
historical studies as Francis Parkman's OREGON TRIAL
(1849) which solidified white attitudes about
manifest destiny and the role of the Indian in the
expanding nation.[2] The single attempt to reconcile
the races in literature used the half-blood as a
transitional figure between civilization and savagery,
but there was a psychological barrier which prevented
such a mythical figure from providing an acceptable
social model which could reconcile the claims of
savagism and civility. Whereas the *idea* of savagism
determined the obligatory treatment of the red race,
the *factual* existence of North and South American
half-bloods was relatively free from similar
long-standing beliefs other than a sometimes vague,
sometimes pronounced, contempt for miscegenation.
Writers devised works which treated the half-blood
Indian in radically different ways than they had
treated the full-blood Indian. The half-blood was
pictured as retaining the worst traits of both races
or as embodying the best traits of both races. In
any case there was normally an uneasiness about the

half-blood which reflected the pervasive social values in white American society and the unreceptiveness to assimilation of people unlike themselves.

The half-bloods objectified in their very being the conflict between the red and white races, and their portrayal in American fiction of the nineteenth century emanates from an uncertainty about their malign or benign relation to society and to their connections with the promises of the new world. The central question which underlies the literary portraits of mixed-blood Indians was whether they represented a new, wonderful natural link between the red and white races or a degenerate, abnormal amalgamation of the worst vices of both races which threatened the promise of a new world civilization. The question was never resolved.[3]

By the end of the nineteenth century, the American Indian was stereotyped most often as the blood-thirsty savage, an image which was perfected in the dime novel and transferred to the Wild West Show. Buffalo Bill was not only the most popular of the dime novel heroes but he was also an extremely successful showman and his Wild West Show toured all over the world, including a crown performance before Queen Victoria. Included among the exhibits in the show were Indians whom Buffalo Bill paraded around in front of the audience and used in the mock battle scenes he staged between the white settlers and the "red men." Buffalo Bill, Pawnee Bill, and Colonel Frederic T. Cummins all used the Indians as entertainers, reenacting their own visions of the "taming of the West." At the same time Indians were being paraded before the public in small towns and villages to sell a variety of medicines and potions, all guaranteed to be "genuine" Indian remedies. Repeatedly the Indian was coopted to make money for white entrepreneurs.

By the time Buffalo Bill and the transient vendors were through, the Indians were firmly established as figures of entertainment like the stage Irishman and the comic Jew.[4] Within this tradition, it was relatively easy to transfer that melodramatic use of the American Indian as an all-around foil for white heroes onto celluloid. And that is precisely what happened. The themes of the dime novels and the traveling shows were adapted to provide the ideas and scripts for the earliest one- and two-reel Westerns and the nineteenth-century image of the Indian was transferred wholesale to the screen.

II

Hollywood fixed rather more firmly those stereotyped images of the Indian and, of course, spread them ever more widely. Where dime novels reached millions of readers, the early films reached tens of millions more including the vast influx of newly arrived immigrants, many of whom could not read English and therefore derived much of their knowledge of the United States from the movies. It gave the filmmakers enormous power to influence public opinion and to form attitudes about the native peoples. In the process the movie makers made money from the films they produced and distributed. Early in the history of the American film the Indian became a staple item of the Saturday-afternoon serial and was from the beginning one of the central icons of the film industry's most prosperous indigenous product--the Western. The appeal of the traditional Western is that it provided clear, simple solutions to complex problems and solidified the triumph of the forces of white civilization. It was ready-made material for films, and the static image of the screen Indian was a readily exploitable commodity. Quickly and unambiguously recognizable in war paint and breechclout, astride his pinto pony, the Indian became the necessary fall guy for the hero, the impediment to progress overcome by the settlers, and finally on an emotional level, the repository of all those age-old, western European bugaboos: irrationality, bestiality, savagism. The American Indian became the ultimate Hollywood stereotype-- easily understood and emotionally necessary--one which provided a universal theme by satisfying the universal fears and uncertainty of the audience. It was an enormously profitable combination.

By the time of World War I the image of the American Indian was well established in the popular film and for the next three decades, with some minor exceptions, that image remained constant. The moviemakers expressed the same uncertainty toward the Indian that the dime novelist and the Puritans had. There was one major difference though: because of the visual nature of the new medium, Hollywood had more opportunity to distort the image of the American Indian. The writers of pulp fiction sketched in the settings and described the "red men," but Hollywood actually showed them. The resulting confusion was symptomatic of white ignorance of the people they had dispossessed. Indians of the Northwest were shown wearing clothing of the Plains Indians and living in dwellings of tribes of the Southwest. Hollywood created the instant Indian: wig, warbonnet, breechclout, moccasins, Hong Kong plastic beadwork. The movies did what thousands of years of social evolution could not do, even what the threat of the encroaching whites did not do: Hollywood produced the homogenized American Indian, devoid of tribal characteristics or regional differences.[5]

Hollywood used the standard images of the Indians, savage, war-like, often noble but vanishing and pathetic, forever locked into a historical past, as integral to the Western experience. For commercial purposes it was necessary to keep the American Indian frozen in this stereotype. So much of America's mythology was contained in the legends of the West and its "taming" that it was emotionally threatening to portray the Indian in any other way. The very experience of the westward movement, the very rationale for the subjugation of the continent depended on this adversary relationship between whites and Indians.

The Indian had a multiple image and at the same time a partial image. _The Indian_--no tribe, no identity, almost always male--was either noble (still savage, but noble nevertheless) or bloodthirsty and vicious. There were variations on the stereotypes--

INTRODUCTION

the drunken Indian, the heathen, the lazy native--but still it was a picture of a creature less than human without religion and lacking in morality or virtue. Usually he was viewed apart from wife or children or any family relationships; he was an isolated figure, one with a pinto pony, gliding across the plains of America, viewed always as an Indian first and an individual last. He combined all the virtues expressed in a Catlin painting with the savagery of a Beadle novel.

From the early days, most Indian roles in film were not played by Indians. This was especially true once the audiences came to recognize the various actors and actresses who helped to establish the star system. The lead parts in films became extremely important for the salability of the property, and practically all leads went to white actors. Really savage Indians were often played by horror film characters such as Bela Lugosi, Lon Chaney, Jr., or Boris Karloff. Often Indians in comic roles were played by stars the audience would recognize as humorous--the Marx Brothers, Buddy Hackett, Joey Bishop, and Buster Keaton. Indians have been played by Latins--Ricardo Montalban and Delores Del Rio, by blacks--Woody Strode, by Japanese--Sessue Hayakawa, and by a variety of box-office giants--Rock Hudson, Elvis Presley, Richard Harris, and Raquel Welch. Indian women often have been portrayed by actors who would gain some measure of sympathy from the audiences--Mary Pickford, Loretta Young, Katherine Ross, Debra Paget, Audrey Hepburn, Julie Newmar, and Donna Reed. Notable examples of using "real" Indians such as Jim Thorp, Chief Walachie, Red Wing, or Chief Thundercloud (the first Tonto) were the exceptions rather than the rule.

With some of the early films, however, notably those of William S. Hart, the filmmakers tried for a realism which led to the employment of Indian actors as extras to provide background atmosphere. But even this trend was not to last for long and during the height of the studio days American Indians were notably absent from films altogether, having been replaced by Hollywood extras hired in and around the studios. What location shooting was done was infrequent. One notable exception was director John Ford, who had a love affair with Monument Valley and for years shot his westerns in this locale, employed members of the Navajo tribe to play the Indians in those films which required American Indians. In spite of the close working relationship between the director and the cast, Ford perpetuated and helped to further develop the exploitative stereotype. It was not until the early 1960s in CHEYENNE AUTUMN (1963) that Ford broke with the Hollywood tradition of simply using American Indians as part of the scenery.

The psychic shock of Viet Nam and its consequences jolted Hollywood out of its apathy and forced the film industry to examine, however clumsily, the stereotypes of the Native Americans. Although the American Indian has long been exploited economically, he has been exploited psychologically even much longer and to much greater extent. Even <u>before</u> settlement of the North American continent, Europeans had definite concepts of the "savages" they would find inhabiting the "wilderness" they were moving into. It was vitally important then, and has remained so for the last 400 years, that the American Indians appear as opponents of civilization and technological progress, backward and primitive in religion and morality, part devil and minion of dark forces of the human soul. They provided the point of comparison against which the more "civilized" Europeans, only lately emerged from a state of semi-savagism, could be measured.

III

What <u>is</u> the current "mythology" of the American Indian? Certainly there are many "mythologies" about the people who were the first to walk the forests, climb the mountains, and plant corn in what is now America. The savage of Beadle dime novels, the romantic nomad of the forest created by Rousseau, the Indian princess with roots in Jamestown and branches as far as Dame Judith Anderson's portrayal in A MAN

INTRODUCTION   xxv

CALLED HORSE, the drunken Indian, the stoic cigar
store vendor, the old chief with the secrets of the
ages in ancient mythology and oral tradition all have
remained as variants of the myth.

    Hollywood has managed to distort and stereotype
almost every ethnic and religious group, but American
Indians seem particularly frozen on screen. Although
a few recent films use a twentieth-century setting,
by and large the Indian of the film exists in a world
somewhere between the landing of the Pilgrims and the
end of the nineteenth century, the primary focus
being on the period between 1850 and 1900, the time
when Indian people were especially desperate in
trying to hold onto their land and were fighting for
their lives. But because this period represents for
non-Indian Americans a time of victory, of overcoming
the final obstacles in the way of progress, it is a
glorified time. To justify mass slaughter and land
grabbing, the movies portrayed Indians as savage and
illiterate, not suited for "modern" civilization.
The few who were descendants of Chingachgook,
Pocahontas, or Squanto were "good" Indians, and they
either "vanished" or were transformed into the Tontos
who knew their place in the changing society.

    Recent films depicting American Indians have
tended to muddy the traditional stereotype, to
reverse, in some cases, the white mythology itself.
That is not to say, however, that the same old images
are not presented in new ways, packaged in new forms.
But a shift in attitudes was accelerated by American
involvement in Viet Nam and the national soul
searching which that war occasioned. The idea that
the government could conceivably commit genocide in
Southeast Asia led some to reconsider the treatment
of the American Indian, our home-territory genocide.
Such close examination produced interesting and at
times thoughtful, if flawed, films. It also
generated new ideas to be exploited as things
"Indian" became fashionable, and BILLY JACK, WHITE
BUFFALO, A MAN CALLED HORSE and its sequel THE RETURN OF
A MAN CALLED HORSE, all to a degree, raised the old
spectre of economic and emotional exploitation.

A number of Indian actors have recently been introduced to film--Chief Dan George, Will Sampson, Ray Tracy, and Geraldine Keams, to name a few. But what of the roles they are consigned to play? Will Sampson, the nearly mute Indian of ONE FLEW OVER THE CUCKOO'S NEST, portrayed a new version of the Indian side-kick and showed that anyone could be a victim of contemporary society. Perhaps his role was more a result of Kesey's vision than of Hollywood's because in his next film, WHITE BUFFALO, Sampson returned to a stereotypical part. Chief Dan George became an instantly popular and believable figure in LITTLE BIG MAN and he was basically non-stereotyped in THE OUTLAW JOSEY WALES, yet in that film the audience was expected to believe that George, playing a Cherokee, could understand the language spoken by the Navajo Geraldine Keams. White actors, however, continue to dominate Indian roles. The Blood people of Alberta put up money for RUNNING BRAVE, the story about Billy Mills, but when the lead was chosen, Robbie Benson got the part. In LEGEND OF WALKS-FAR-WOMAN, Raquel Welch plays the leading female role while Indian actors such as Geraldine Keams play minor parts. In WINDWALKER, generally a sensitive film which used Crow language with subtitles in English and many fine Indian actors, the lead was played by the British actor Trevor Howard.

What will happen to the image of the Indian in film in the future is impossible to predict. If past history is any guide, films will find or develop another stereotype, one that will accommodate a new popular image. Mass arts tend to the allegorical, which allows them a broader or more universal appeal, preferring surfaces and types to essences and individuals. While we can expect to see American Indians portrayed more sympathetically and with greater historical accuracy, the Indian in the popular film will no doubt remain as one-dimensional as all other types.

Notes

[1] For a fuller discussion, see Roy Harvey Pearce, SAVAGISM AND CIVILIZATION: A STUDY OF THE INDIAN AND THE AMERICAN MIND (Baltimore: Johns Hopkins University Press, 1965); Richard Slotkin, REGENERATION THROUGH VIOLENCE: THE MYTHOLOGY OF THE AMERICAN FRONTIER, 1600-1860 (Middletown, CT: Wesleyan University Press, 1973); Leslie Fiedler, THE RETURN OF THE VANISHING AMERICAN (New York: Stein and Day, 1969); Bernard Sheehan, SAVAGISM AND CIVILITY: INDIANS AND ENGLISHMEN IN COLONIAL VIRGINIA (Cambridge, England: Cambridge University Press, 1980).

[2] Louise K. Barnett, THE IGNOBLE SAVAGE: AMERICAN LITERARY RACISM (Westport, CT: Greenwood Press, 1975).

[3] William J. Scheick, THE HALF-BLOOD: A CULTURAL SYMBOL IN 19TH CENTURY AMERICAN FICTION (Lexington: University of Kentucky, 1979).

[4] See, for example, Robert F. Berkhofer, Jr., THE WHITE MAN'S INDIAN (New York: Vintage Books, 1979); Raymond William Stedman, SHADOWS OF THE INDIAN: STEREOTYPES IN AMERICAN CULTURE (Norman: University of Oklahoma Press, 1982).

[5] Additional information about the development of the Indian image in film can be found in Gretchen Bataille and Charles L. P. Silet, THE PRETEND INDIANS: IMAGES OF NATIVE AMERICANS IN THE MOVIES (Ames: Iowa State University Press, 1980); Ralph and Natasha Friar, THE ONLY GOOD INDIAN . . .: THE HOLLYWOOD GOSPEL (New York: Drama Book Specialists, 1972).

General Background

General Background

1. American Indian Historical Society. COMMON MIS-
   CONCEPTIONS ABOUT AMERICAN INDIANS. San Francisco: Indian Historian Press, 1967.

   Jeannette Costo, editor of THE INDIAN HISTORIAN,
   explains the purpose of this small book: to point
   out origins of misconceptions about American
   Indians and provide source materials to correct
   the ethnic falsehoods.

2. Barnett, Louise K. THE IGNOBLE SAVAGE: AMERICAN
   LITERARY RACISM, 1790-1890. Westport, CT:
   Greenwood Press, 1975.

   Traces a hundred years' stereotyping of American
   Indians in captivity narratives, frontier romances,
   and Puritan chronicles. Includes a listing of
   frontier romances and a bibliography.

3. Barry, Roxana. "Rousseau, Buffalo Bill and the
   European Image of the American Indian." ART
   NEWS, 74 (Dec. 1975): 58-61.

   Examines the portrayal of the Indian as a noble
   savage in the art of the late nineteenth century.
   She is most concerned with the work of sculptors
   and the aesthetic movement which stimulated the
   portrait of the Indian as a noble savage.

4. Bataille, Gretchen M. "Education and the Images of the American Indian." EXPLORATIONS IN ETHNIC STUDIES, 1 (Jan. 1978): 37-49.

   Discusses the popular images of the American Indian and the stereotypes perpetuated through educational materials.

5. Beidler, Peter G., and Marion F. Egge. THE AMERICAN INDIAN IN SHORT FICTION: AN ANNOTATED BIBLIOGRAPHY. Metuchen, NJ: Scarecrow Press, 1979.

   Contains a useful index with 880 annotated entries of short stories about Indians which have appeared in books and magazines since 1890.

6. Berkhofer, Robert F., Jr. THE WHITE MAN'S INDIAN. New York: Alfred A. Knopf, 1978.

   Draws from early journals of explorers and missionaries, anthropological texts, literature, and art to demonstrate the changes in white attitudes toward Indians through time and the effects of the attitudes on political and social policies.

7. Black, Nancy B., and Bette S. Weidman. WHITE ON RED: IMAGES OF THE AMERICAN INDIAN. Port Washington, NY: Kennikat Press, 1976.

   A collection of excerpts from Captain John Smith (1624) to Helen Hunt Jackson (1884) which demonstrates various white views of Indians ranging from openly hostile to romantic and sympathetic accounts.

8. Byler, Mary Gloyne. "The Image of American Indians Projected by Non-Indian Writers." LIBRARY JOURNAL, 99 (Feb. 15, 1974): 546-549.

Points out that non-Indian writers have often unconsciously attacked Indians through the use of language and cultural assumptions underpinning the language.

9. Coen, Rena Neumann. THE RED MAN IN ART. Minneapolis: Lerner Publications, 1972.

    Deals with the images of American Indians in painting and sculpture as symbols in art created by both Indians and non-Indians.

10. Costo, Rupert, and Jeannette Henry. TEXTBOOKS AND THE AMERICAN INDIAN. San Francisco: Indian Historian Press, 1970.

    Outlines what most history books omit or distort about American Indian history, evaluates over 300 books, and offers suggestions for improvement of curricula.

11. Drinnon, Richard. FACING WEST: THE METAPHYSICS OF INDIAN-HATING AND EMPIRE BUILDING. Minneapolis: University of Minnesota Press, 1980.

    Discusses both the friends and detractors of American Indians from early accounts to the influence of the frontier mentality on twentieth-century politics. An extensive bibliographical essay is useful to anyone doing research on the history of Indian images.

12. Ducheneaux, Franklin. "The American Indian: Beyond the Stereotypes." TODAY'S EDUCATION, 62 (May 1973): 22-24.

    Discusses the dual image of the Indian, "noble savage or the bloodthirsty, dirty red-skin," as well as newer mass-media images. Also gives a realistic portrayal of Indians in today's society.

13. Ewers, John. "The Emergence of the Plains Indian as the Symbol of the North America Indian." ANNUAL REPORT. Smithsonian Institute. Washington, DC: USGPO, 1964.

    Examines the image of the Plains Indian on coins, in official photographs, and in popular culture.

14. Ewers, John C. "The Static Images" in LOOK TO THE MOUNTAINTOP. Ed. Robert Iocopi. San Jose, CA: Gousha Publications, 1972. Pp. 107-109.

    Traces the many media images of American Indians which have appeared and continue to appear despite their inconsistency with reality.

15. Gerdts, W.H. "The Marble Savage." ART IN AMERICA, 62 (July 1974): 64-70.

    Discusses nineteenth-century sculpture of the American Indian, examining the classical figure which evolved into a more aboriginal figure as attitudes toward Indians changed.

16. Glasrud, Bruce A., and Alan M. Smith, eds. RACE RELATIONS IN BRITISH NORTH AMERICA, 1607-1783. Chicago: Nelson-Hall, 1982.

    Presents views of white, red, and black relationships on the Atlantic coast during the pre-revolutionary and revolutionary periods. There are essays on the Iroquois, "playing Indians," Indian agriculture, and the effects of the Revolutionary War on Southern Indians.

GENERAL BACKGROUND   7

17. Howard, James H. "The Native American Image in
     Western Europe." AMERICAN INDIAN QUARTERLY, 4
     (Feb. 1978): 33-56.

     This comparative study of United States and
     Western European attitudes toward the Indian
     examines museums, ethnic enclaves in Europe,
     and views of European cultural anthropologists.

18. Hudson, Charles M., ed. RED, WHITE, AND BLACK:
     SYMPOSIUM ON INDIANS IN THE OLD SOUTH. Athens:
     University of Georgia Press, 1971.

     This collection of papers from the Southern
     Anthropological Society attempts to fill the gaps
     in southern history and anthropology by focusing
     on Indians and blacks rather than whites. Although
     limited to the South, this book provides specific
     essays on the relationships among the races in
     the Old South. Essays cover language, maps,
     archeological findings, politics, and the social
     order.

19. Jennings, Francis. THE INVASION OF AMERICA:
     INDIANS, COLONIALISM AND THE CANT OF CONQUEST.
     New York: W.W. Norton, 1975.

     Approaches the colonization of America from the
     American Indian perspective.

20. Johannsen, Albert. THE HOUSE OF BEADLE AND ADAMS.
     Norman: University of Oklahoma Press, 1950.

     This review of dime novels demonstrates the
     nineteenth-century sources of many twentieth-
     century Indian stereotypes.

21. Josephy, Alvin M., Jr. "The Splendid Indians of
     Edward S. Curtis." AMERICAN HERITAGE, 25

(Feb. 1974): 40-59.

Discusses a unique set of photographs by Curtis whom he describes as sensitive and who demonstrated deep ethnic feeling and artistry in his early photographs.

22. Keiser, Albert. THE INDIAN IN AMERICAN LITERATURE. New York: Oxford University Press, 1933.

    A classic study tracing the Indian in literature from Pocahontas through the twentieth century.

23. LaRoque, Emma. DEFEATHERING THE INDIAN. Agincourt, Canada: The Book Society of Canada, 1975.

    Describes the author's experiences growing up as a Metis woman in Canada who encountered stereotypes of Indians in the schools and in her interactions with non-Indians. This is a personal account with suggestions for "destereotyping" the Indian.

24. Lopez, Andres. PAGANS IN OUR MIDST. Rooseveltown, NY: Akwesasne Notes, n.d.

    A collection of printed accounts and visual representations of American Indians between 1885 and 1910 documenting the popular images and attitudes in newspapers, magazines, and official reports dealing with the Iroquois.

25. Lyman, Christopher M. THE VANISHING RACE AND OTHER ILLUSIONS: PHOTOGRAPHS OF INDIANS BY EDWARD S. CURTIS. New York: Pantheon, 1982.

    This exhibition catalog includes an introduction by Vine Deloria, Jr., and several excellent essays on the Indian stereotype created by photographers and the images Curtis created in his posed pictures of American Indians.

26. McNickle, D'Arcy. "American Indians Who Never Were." INDIAN HISTORIAN, 3 (Summer 1970): 4-7.

    McNickle is critical of anthropological generalizations about American Indians which are inaccurate and predicts that American Indians will maintain strong ties to the past and the values of their cultures.

27. Murphy, Sharon. "American Indians and the Media: Neglect and Stereotype." JOURNALISM HISTORY, 6 (1979): 39-43.

    Reviews misrepresentation in the print media as well as films. She cites examples from nineteenth-century newspaper coverage up to reports of Wounded Knee in 1973.

28. Nash, Gary B. RED, WHITE AND BLACK: THE PEOPLES OF EARLY AMERICA. Englewood Cliffs, NJ: Prentice-Hall, Inc., 1974.

    A broad general treatment of European-Indian relations, this book provides an excellent introduction to the kinds of images which arose from the early conflicts between American Indians and whites and the text suggests some of the historical reasons behind the stereotyping and image fixing.

29. Noschese, Christine. "The Ethnic Image in the Media." CIVIL RIGHTS DIGEST, 11 (Fall 1978): 28-34.

    Focuses on European white ethnics and gives

examples from television commercials of how the media show "one perception of what the real American wants to be." Noschese concludes that, although more non-white ethnic persons now appear in the media, they are still in stereotypical roles or their ethnicity is disguised to make them appear as mainstream white Americans.

30. Parry, Ellwood. THE IMAGE OF THE INDIAN AND THE BLACK MAN IN AMERICAN ART, 1590-1900. New York: George Braziller, 1974.

    Discusses and illustrates the iconography of the New World and the images that have depicted Indians and blacks in popular culture as well as high art between 1590 and 1900.

31. Pearce, Roy Harvey. SAVAGISM AND CIVILIZATION: A STUDY OF THE INDIAN AND THE AMERICAN MIND. Baltimore: Johns Hopkins Press, 1965 (orig. THE SAVAGES OF AMERICA: A STUDY OF THE INDIAN AND THE IDEA OF CIVILIZATION, 1953).

    Pearce's classic study of "the history of a belief"--that civilized people saw in the Indian all that was savage and must be overcome--is an important document in the study of the American Indian image. He analyzes the origins as well as the expressions of the ideas of savagism and civilization in American thought and culture.

32. Russell, Don. THE WILD WEST: A HISTORY OF THE WILD WEST SHOWS. Dallas: Amon Carter Museum of Western Art, 1970.

    The late nineteenth- and early twentieth-century traveling exhibitions of the "Wild West" did much to create and perpetuate the Indian image. Russell discusses Buffalo Bill as well as Pawnee Bill and the others. Bibliography included.

GENERAL BACKGROUND   11

33. Sando, Joe S. "White Created Myths About the
     American Indian." INDIAN HISTORIAN, 4 (Winter
     1971): 10-11.

     Review of the stereotypes of American Indians
     that have become standard elements in the Hollywood
     Western--scalping, laziness, battles/massacres, and
     the influences of the missionaries and the government.

34. Savage, William W., Jr., ed. INDIAN LIFE: TRANS-
     FORMING AN AMERICAN MYTH. Norman: University
     of Nebraska Press, 1977.

     Illustrated collection of essays and excerpts
     which focus on attitudes about Indians between
     1882 and 1914. Includes military, governmental,
     and literary views.

35. Scheick, William J. THE HALF-BLOOD: A CULTURAL
     SYMBOL IN 19TH CENTURY AMERICAN FICTION. Lexington: University Press of Kentucky, 1979.

     The half-blood is a dramatic symbol of the integration of whites and Indians and as such has been
     variously portrayed as embodying both good and bad
     traits of the races. Scheick focuses on nineteenth-century popular fiction in his examination
     of the half-blood as a cultural symbol.

36. Scholder, Fritz. INDIAN KITSCH: THE USE AND
     MISUSE OF INDIAN IMAGES. Flagstaff, AZ: Northland Press, 1979.

     Artist Scholder has collected a number of popular culture Indian images to visually demonstrate
     the pervasiveness of stereotypes.

37. Schwartz, Joseph. "The Wild West Show: Everything

Genuine." JOURNAL OF POPULAR CULTURE, 3 (Spring 1970): 656-666.

Concludes that the lasting popularity of the Wild West shows was based on a combination of authenticity and theatrics. As the West changed, the show began to lose its cultural authenticity and the popularity waned.

38. Sell, Henry B., and Victor Weyright. BUFFALO BILL AND THE WILD WEST. New York: Oxford University Press, 1955.

Traces the origin of Buffalo Bill's Wild West Show and provides the background information for the importance of the show both in America and abroad. There is brief mention of the one film Buffalo Bill appeared in. Also discussed is the way in which the whole idea of the "Wild West" came to have an influence on the popular mind of the late nineteenth century.

39. Shaughnessy, Tim. "White Stereotypes of Indians." JOURNAL OF AMERICAN INDIAN EDUCATION, 17 (Jan. 1978): 20-24.

After defining ethnic stereotype, Shaughnessy points out examples and ends with a plea that American Indians be treated on the basis of individual achievements and errors.

40. Slotkin, Richard. REGENERATION THROUGH VIOLENCE: THE MYTHOLOGY OF THE AMERICAN FRONTIER, 1600-1860. Middletown, CT: Wesleyan University Press, 1973.

Analyzes the "myths" that have undergirded the European-American struggles with the American Indian and the frontier experience. He discusses captivity narratives, Indian wars, and early novels.

41. Smith, Robert C. "The Noble Savage in Paintings and Prints." ANTIQUES, 74 (July 1958): 57-59.

    Points out that "true" representations of the Indian in the art of the nineteenth century are rare. The Indian is often caught in the artistic tradition of the time, classicism or romanticism, and is rarely presented realistically.

42. Stedman, Raymond William. SHADOWS OF THE INDIAN: STEREOTYPES IN AMERICAN CULTURE. Norman: University of Oklahoma Press, 1982.

    Examines the stereotypes of American Indians in literature, art, and popular culture, tracing the images from early explorers' journals to contemporary films. Illustrations support his thesis that the Indian has most often been presented unrealistically.

43. Takaki, Ronald T. IRON CAGES: RACE AND CULTURE IN NINETEENTH-CENTURY AMERICA. New York: Alfred A. Knopf, 1979.

    Analyzes the relationships among blacks, Indians, Mexicans, and Asians in relation to political, social, and economic developments in the United States.

44. Tenkate, Herman F.C. "The Indian in Literature." INDIAN HISTORIAN, 3 (Summer 1970): 12-32.

    Surveys literature between 1799 and 1916, describing the literary treatments which have molded the various Indian stereotypes.

45. Trenner, Robert A. "Popular Images and the American Indian: A Centennial View." NEW MEXICO HISTORICAL REVIEW, 60 (July 1976): 215-232.

The 1876 view of the Indian was that of a savage, cruel, and inhuman being worthy of curiosity. This view was generated in the literature of the day and became a dominant white cultural assumption with an impact on public policy.

46. Van Der Beets, Richard. "A Surfeit of Style: The Indian Captivity Narrative as Penny Dreadful." RESEARCH STUDIES, 39 (Dec. 1971): 297-306.

    The captivity narrative progressed from inspiration toward patriotism to cheap thriller inspiring horror. It was used to manipulate the attitudes of Americans toward Indians and generated hatred and fear.

47. Vaughan, Alden T. NEW ENGLAND FRONTIER: PURITANS AND INDIANS, 1620-1675. New York: W.W. Norton, 1979.

    A revisionist study of the Puritan-Indian relationships in which Vaughan argues that the Puritans did initially attempt to deal fairly with the Indians.

48. Vinson, J. Chal. THOMAS NAST: POLITICAL CARTOONIST. Athens: University of Georgia Press, 1967.

    The nineteenth-century cartoonist often used the stereotypes of Indians to communicate his political perspective. The book includes 154 examples of Nast's work.

49. Vogel, Virgil. THE INDIAN IN AMERICAN HISTORY. Evanston, IL: Integrated Education Associates, 1968.

    In this pamphlet Vogel discusses obliteration, defamation, disembodiment, and disparagement as the four means by which historians have created or perpetuated false images of American Indians.

50. Wilson, Charles Reagan. "Racial Reservations: Indians and Blacks in American Magazines, 1865-1900." JOURNAL OF POPULAR CULTURE, 10 (Summer 1976): 70-79.

    Both Indians and blacks were seen negatively because they did not conform to Anglo-Saxon patterns. Between 1865 and 1900 Indians appeared to be treated more favorably than blacks, although Wilson concludes that currently they are in a less advantageous position.

Articles and Books on
American Indians in Films

Articles and Books on
American Indians in Film

51. "A 1914 Movie Review." AKWESASNE NOTES, 5 (Early Winter 1973): 14.

    This reprint from MOVING PICTURE WORLD is one of the earliest comments on the portrayal of the Indian in film and underscores the fact that from the beginnings of the industry the Indian has been an important subject for films.

52. "Accuracy in Indian Subjects." MOVING PICTURE WORLD, 5 (July 10, 1909): 48.

    This early article discusses the exaggerated acting styles and misrepresentation of the Indians in the first films.

53. "Brando Refuses Oscar." AKWESASNE NOTES, 5 (Late Summer 1973): 10.

    Discusses Brando's views of the use of Indians in films as "a perennial bad force--a malignant source of evil." The text of his speech refusing the Academy Award is included as are reactions of several journalists to the incident.

54. "Hollywood's Revenge." TIME, 101 (April 9, 1973): 54.

Comments on Sacheen Littlefeather, an Apache actress, who appeared at the Academy Awards to reject Marlon Brando's Oscar and deliver a political speech.

55. "Indians and the Media: A Panel Discussion." CIVIL RIGHTS DIGEST, 6 (Feb. 1973): 41-45.

   Condensed transcript from a panel discussion that focused on media communications as they relate to the Indian people of the United States.

56. "Indians Grieve Over Picture Shows." MOVING PICTURE WORLD, 10 (Oct. 7, 1911): 32.

   Makes the point that contemporary Indians are peacefully engaged in farming and, although they are avid movie fans, it is greatly disturbing to them to be so unjustly pictured in films.

57. "Indians War on Films: Delegation at Washington to Protest Against Alleged Libels in Moving Pictures." MOVING PICTURE WORLD, 8 (March 18, 1911): 581.

   A Chippewa delegation joined other tribes in an "uprising" against the use of whites dressed up as Indians in moving pictures. The group denounced these films as giving an untrue picture of the Indian.

58. "The 'Make-Believe' Indian." MOVING PICTURE WORLD, 8 (March 4, 1911): 473.

   Criticizes motion pictures for not accurately portraying the Indians as a "noble race of people, with their splendid physique and physical prowess." They hope a series of films of "real" Indian life will be forthcoming.

ARTICLES AND BOOKS

59. "Vogue of Western and Military Drama." MOVING PICTURE WORLD, 9 (August 5, 1911): 271-272.

   Deals with the appeal of the Westerns as Man vs. Nature and states that feeling toward the "red man" has changed in the last century, that he is no longer hated or feared, but admired for his noble qualities and envied for his closeness to nature. This desire to do the Indian belated justice runs through early Indian films and accounts for their popularity.

60. Aitken, Will. "Histrionics." TAKE ONE, 5 (1976): 39.

   Compares BUFFALO BILL AND THE INDIANS to NASHVILLE and other films Robert Altman has directed.

61. Ames, Katrine, and Martin Kasindorf. "Big Will." NEWSWEEK, 87 (July 26, 1976): 73.

   Presents a brief biographical sketch of Will Sampson, Creek Indian, who acted in BUFFALO BILL AND THE INDIANS and ONE FLEW OVER THE CUCKOO'S NEST. Sampson comments, "All the Indians' heroes are long dead. We don't have today's heroes like white people. Indians are a proud people, but we can't say Crazy Horse is going to win the World Series."

62. Balshofer, Fred J., and Arthur C. Miller. ONE REEL A WEEK. Berkeley: University of California Press, 1967.

   Autobiographical account of two cinematographers includes several chapters on the filming of Westerns.

63. Bataille, Gretchen. "Interview with N. Scott

Momaday." STUDIES IN AMERICAN INDIAN LITERA-
TURES, 4 (1980): 1-3.

Interview with Momaday about his Pulitzer
Prize-winning novel, HOUSE MADE OF DAWN, which was
adapted for the screen. His role as consultant is
discussed.

64. Bataille, Gretchen M., and Charles L.P. Silet.
"A Checklist of Published Materials on Popular
Images of the Indian in the American Film."
THE JOURNAL OF POPULAR FILM, 5 (1976): 171-182.

Annotated compilation of books, articles, and
reviews which deal with the images of American
Indians in films.

65. Bataille, Gretchen M., and Charles L.P. Silet.
"Economic and Psychic Exploitation of American Indians." EXPLORATIONS IN ETHNIC STUDIES,
6 (July 1983): 8-21.

Presents examples to demonstrate that the motion
picture industry is part of a long tradition of
exploitation of American Indians. More devastating
than economic exploitation, however, is the psychic
exploitation which has robbed Indian people of their
sense of self.

66. Bataille, Gretchen M., and Charles L.P. Silet.
"The Entertaining Anachronism: Indians in Ameri-
can Film" in THE KALEIDOSCOPIC LENS: HOW HOLLY-
WOOD VIEWS ETHNIC GROUPS. Ed. Randall M. Miller.
Englewood, NJ: Jerome S. Ozer, Pub., 1980. Pp.
36-53.

Traces the Indian image that was developed on
film by looking at early examples in dime novels
and captivity narratives. The authors cite recent
films and studies of American Indian participation

in the filmmaking process, noting that change is slow and it will take a concerted effort to redefine the images that are so firmly a part of the film tradition.

67. Bataille, Gretchen M., and Charles L.P. Silet. THE PRETEND INDIANS: IMAGES OF NATIVE AMERICANS IN THE MOVIES. Ames: Iowa State University Press, 1980.

    In this collection of essays and film reviews, the authors trace the precursors of the Hollywood image and examine how various writers have explored the Indian images. Introduction by Vine Deloria, Jr.

68. Beale, Lewis. "The American Way West." FILMS AND FILMING, 18 (April 1972): 24-30.

    Criticizes Hollywood's attempt to correct the stereotype of the Indian as shifting too far in the direction of showing all Indians to be good and all whites to be evil.

69. Blakey, Carla M. "The American Indian in Films, Part I." FILM NEWS, 27 (Sept. 1970): 6-10.

    The first of a two-part series, this article examines several films, mostly documentaries, about Indians.

70. Blakey, Carla M. "The American Indian in Films, Part II." FILM NEWS, 27 (Oct. 1970): 6-11.

    In the second part of the series, Blakey continues to review films suitable for classroom use.

71. Boyd, David. "Prisoner of the Night." FILM HERALD, 12 (1976-1977): 24-30.

Discusses the influence of Ford's THE SEARCHERS on TAXI DRIVER, comparing the wilderness of Monument Valley to the urban frontier of the inner city. Scar, the Comanche chief in THE SEARCHERS, is compared to Sport, the pimp in Scorsese's film.

72. Brascoupe, Simon. "What Is an Indian? What Is a Stereotype?" TURTLE, 3 (Summer 1981): 2-3.

    Historical analysis of the precursors of film stereotypes with brief reviews of several contemporary films.

73. Brauer, Ralph, and Donna Brauer. THE HORSE, THE GUN, AND THE PIECE OF PROPERTY: CHANGING IMAGES OF THE TV WESTERN. Bowling Green, OH: Bowling Green University Popular Press, 1975.

    Includes one chapter on the portrayal of minorities in the television Western and underscores the similarity of negative portrayals on television and in the movies.

74. Brownlow, Kevin. THE WAR, THE WEST, AND THE WILDERNESS. New York: Alfred A. Knopf, 1979.

    This study of early filmmakers contains a great deal of information about how the Indian was depicted in early films and is especially helpful because the volume contains vintage photographs.

75. Bush, W. Stephen. "Moving Picture Absurdities." MOVING PICTURE WORLD, 9 (Sept. 16, 1911): 773.

    Laments the typical depiction of the Indian, always squinting as if he needed glasses, either wholly good and the white man's friend, or totally evil and fiendish. The writer believes audiences are tiring of this stereotype.

76. Calder, Jenni. THERE MUST BE A LONE RANGER. London: Hamish Hamilton, 1974.

    Devotes an entire chapter to the Indian's portrayal in Hollywood movies. Most of her comments refer to films from the 1930s to the 1970s.

77. Calder-Marshall, Arthur. THE INNOCENT EYE: THE LIFE OF ROBERT J. FLAHERTY. London: W.H. Allen, 1963.

    Includes a description of the making of NANOOK OF THE NORTH and the conflict between reality and Flaherty's romantic views of native peoples.

78. California Advisory Committee to the U.S. Commission on Civil Rights. BEHIND THE SCENES: EQUAL EMPLOYMENT OPPORTUNITY IN THE MOTION PICTURE INDUSTRY. Washington, DC: USGPO, 1978.

    Detailed study of employment statistics and affirmative action in major Hollywood studios; includes employment statistics of American Indians.

79. Carpenter, Edmund. "Film, Primitive Man, and Reality." MEDIA ECOLOGY REVIEW, 2 (Summer-Fall 1973): 2-4.

    Presents a general view of indigenous peoples and their portrayal in the media.

80. Cawelti, John G. "Cowboys, Indians, Outlaws." AMERICAN WEST, 1 (Spring 1964): 28-35, 77-79.

    Sees the Westerns of novels, movies, and television as a direct elaboration of the Buffalo

Bill Wild West Show and dime novels. The basic
elements in the myth of the West came from the
period between 1850 and 1870.

81. Cawelti, John G. "Reflections on the New Western
Films: The Jewish Cowboy, the Black Avenger, and
the Return of the Vanishing American." THE
UNIVERSITY OF CHICAGO MAGAZINE, 65 (Jan.-Feb.
1973): 25-32.

Argues that the films are setting forth a new
myth about the West, one which incorporates a
contemporary and changing attitude toward American Indians. This new myth amounts to a complete
reversal of the symbolic meanings ascribed to major
groups in the Western. The hero is regenerated
through his contact with the native inhabitants,
the pioneers become the bad guys and the Indians
the force for good. The cavalry, once a symbol of
rescue and law and order, becomes "the instrument
of brutal massacre."

82. Cawelti, John. THE SIX-GUN MYSTIQUE. Bowling
Green, OH: Bowling Green University Popular
Press, 1973.

The American Indian is treated as part of a
broader analysis of the Western genre and its
characteristics in both popular fiction and in
film.

83. Churchill, Ward. "Film Stereotyping of Native
Americans." BOOK FORUM, 5 (1981): 370-375.

Reviews the ways in which films have misrepresented American Indians by locking them into a
limited time period (1825-1880), by defining
Indian culture with Euro-American value systems,
and by ignoring tribal differences in language,
costume, and customs.

84. Churchill, Ward, Norbert Hill, and Mary Ann Hill. "Media Stereotyping and Native Response: An Historical Overview." THE INDIAN HISTORIAN, 11 (Dec. 1978): 45-56, 63.

    Contains an historical overview of the stereotypes of the Indian in the American film plus an analysis of similar stereotyping in other media.

85. Clark, Joan. "Some Wrongs Righted on Film: Vanishing American: Part I." FILM LIBRARY QUARTERLY, 3 (Winter 1969-70): 27, 47.

    Reviews four films good for classroom use: THE BALLAD OF CROWFOOT, THE END OF THE TRAIL, MASS FOR THE DAKOTA SIOUX, and NOW THAT THE BUFFALO ARE GONE.

86. Corliss, Richard. "Red Hot and Medium Cool." NATIONAL REVIEW, 22 (Jan. 13, 1970): 41-43.

    Writes that the Indian has finally made it onto the list of liberal causes just behind blacks, homosexuals, and women, but TELL THEM WILLIE BOY IS HERE skips "the facile moralizing that would convert the Indian into a totem of white guilt; the leading character is . . . something more: an individual, and not as the collective hero, whether benign or rabid, or a long-silent minority."

87. Dench, Ernest Alfred. "The Dangers of Employing Redskins as Movie Actors" in MAKING THE MOVIES. New York: Macmillan, 1915. Pp. 92-94.

    In an early article about Indians employed as actors, Dench says, "The Red Indians who have been fortunate enough to secure permanent engagements with the several Western film companies are paid a salary that keeps them well provided with tobacco and their worshipped 'firewater.'"

88. Denton, James F. "The Red Man Plays Indian."
COLLIERS, 113 (March 18, 1944): 18-19.

   The Navajos portray the Plains tribes in the new film BUFFALO BILL and find the transition both difficult and comical. The Indian actors are described as being primarily interested in the money they are earning with little or no concern for the historical accuracy of the film.

89. Dervin, Daniel A. "Creativity and Collaboration in Three American Movies." AMERICAN IMAGO, 34 (Summer 1977): 179-203.

   Discusses HUSTLE, ALICE DOESN'T LIVE HERE ANYMORE, and LITTLE BIG MAN. In discussing LITTLE BIG MAN, Dervin sees the film as interpreting recent history, the American Indian Movement, and the Vietnam War. LITTLE BIG MAN is also a result of Penn's awareness of Freud, Erickson, and the insights of psychoanalysis.

90. DiMino, Angelo V. "Stop Stereotyping Indian Studies: Filming Seneca History." INSTRUCTOR, 82 (Nov. 1972): 100-103.

   A short essay on how some fifth-grade students shot their own movie of Seneca life and history.

91. Dodi, Steve. "Restoring Robert Flaherty's NANOOK OF THE NORTH." FILM LIBRARY QUARTERLY, 10 (1977): 7-20.

   Discusses the original documentary and the reissue of it as a sound film.

92. Eiselein, E.B. THREE REPORTS ON SERVING NATIVE AMERICAN BROADCAST NEEDS. Lincoln, NE: Native American Public Broadcasting Consortium, 1982.

These three reports include the following: Native Americans and Broadcasting, Serving Native American Media Needs, and Public Broadcasting and Native Americans.

93. Elrod, Norman, and Alexander Weber. "Indian Film Seminar in Switzerland." WASSAJA, 3 (July 1975): 15.

    Comment on some of the films shown in Switzerland from the perspective that they are images of class struggles depicting racial problems.

94. Emmens, Carol A. "Navajo, the Last Red Indians." FILM LIBRARY QUARTERLY, 6 (Fall 1973): 46.

    Review of a BBC-TV and Time-Life documentary on the Navajo.

95. Erens, Patricia. "Images of Minority and Foreign Groups in American Films: 1958-73." JUMP-CUT, 7 (May-July 1975): 19-22.

    Contains an introductory note to an annotated bibliography of source materials dealing with minority groups in the film. The author makes a convincing argument for studying the Western.

96. Everson, William. A PICTORIAL HISTORY OF THE WESTERN FILM. New York: Citadel Press, 1969.

    Includes little on American Indians except comments about the reliable theme--"stirring up the Indians"--which appears repeatedly in the Western movie.

97. Everson, W.K. "Sun Valley Western Film Conference." FILMS IN REVIEW, 27 (Oct. 1976): 477, 483.

Contains a discussion of the conference including sessions on the Indian in film. The article presents comments about Indian responses to those films.

98. Eyles, Allen. THE WESTERN: AN ILLUSTRATED GUIDE. New York: A.S. Barnes & Co., 1967.

   This encyclopedic guide to the Western contains scattered references to Indian actors (Jay Silverheels), Indian characters (Sitting Bull), and directors who made films about Indians (John Ford).

99. Fenin, George N. "The Western--Old and New." FILM CULTURE, 2 (Winter 1956): 7-10.

   Dealing primarily with the Western myth and focusing on the cowboy, Fenin treats the Indian as part of the sagebrush which, along with the bison, had to be cleared from the plains before the pioneers could inhabit them. There is a brief mention of Hollywood's efforts at historical accuracy in portraying American Indians in the fifties.

100. Fenin, George N., and William K. Everson. THE WESTERN: FROM SILENTS TO THE SEVENTIES. New York: Grossman Publishers, 1973.

   Traces the image of the Indian from early films to the present, pointing out the various images of the "senseless bloodthirsty savage" and the "dignified original American." They comment that the Indian was "alternately villainous and misunderstood, but he rarely emerged as a human being."

101. Florence, William R. "John Ford . . . the Duke . . . and Monument Valley." ARIZONA HIGHWAYS,

57 (Sept. 1981): 22-37.

Ford made nine films in Monument Valley on the Navajo Reservation, beginning with STAGECOACH in 1939 and ending with CHEYENNE AUTUMN in 1964. This illustrated article discusses Ford's use of the Valley.

102. Folsom, James K. "'Western' Themes and Western Films." WESTERN AMERICAN LITERATURE, 2 (Fall 1967): 195-203.

    Elaborates on the "good" Indian and the "bad" Indian and reminds us of the cinematic cliche-- a wagon train in a circle around the campfire with children playing and the men keeping guard; an owl hoots, but we all know it's really an Indian and an attack is soon to come.

103. Franklin, Eliza. "Westerns, First, and Lasting." QUARTERLY OF FILM, RADIO, AND TELEVISION, 7 (Winter 1952): 109-115.

    A review of Westerns from the beginning; includes brief comments on the role of Indians as often looking "silly." Contains discussion of the content of the films, audiences, and changing popularity.

104. French, Philip. "The Indian in the Western Movie." ART IN AMERICA, 60 (July-August 1972): 32-39.

    Concentrates on the image of the Indian in films since 1950, the "watershed year" for Western movies.

105. French, Philip. WESTERNS: ASPECTS OF A MOVIE GENRE. London: Secker and Warburg, 1973.

Sees 1950 as the year that marked a change in the treatment of the Indian in the Westerns; traces the images from early films such as THE MASSACRE through the sixties, noting always that the Indian is used as "more of a symbol, less an individual" than are other characters in the Western movie.

106. French, Philip. WESTERNS: ASPECTS OF A MOVIE GENRE. New York: Oxford University Press, 1977. Pp. 76-99.

In his chapter "Indians and Blacks," French writes of the prejudices that have appeared on screen and surveys films from the 1950s to the early 1970s.

107. Friar, Ralph. "White Man Speaks With a Split Tongue, Forked Tongue, Tongue of Snake." FILM LIBRARY QUARTERLY, 3 (Winter 1969-1970): 16-23.

Friar condenses the material and ideas presented in his longer study of the Indian in film, THE ONLY GOOD INDIAN . . .: THE HOLLYWOOD GOSPEL. He discusses some of the more significant films and comments on Kopit's play INDIANS--a production which reverses the earlier images and results in equally inaccurate stereotyping.

108. Friar, Ralph E., and Natasha A. Friar. THE ONLY GOOD INDIAN . . .: THE HOLLYWOOD GOSPEL. New York: Drama Book Specialists, 1972.

Comprehensive study of the Indian in film. The Friars append a lengthy list of films categorizing the various ways in which Indians functioned in the movies. They also provide several stills and miscellaneous material such as promotional information for the films. They bring in related material such as popular literature, songs, and

Wild West shows--all of which influenced the portrayal of the Indian in the Hollywood movie.

109. Georgakas, Dan. "They Have Not Spoken: American Indians in Film." FILM QUARTERLY, 25 (Spring 1972): 26-32.

    Takes a serious look at the flaws in A MAN CALLED HORSE, SOLDIER BLUE, LITTLE BIG MAN, and TELL THEM WILLIE BOY IS HERE.

110. Goodman, Ezra. "Hollywood and Minorities." ASIA AND THE AMERICAS, 43 (Jan. 1943): 34-35.

    Reviews treatment of East Indians, blacks, Russians, American Indians, Chinese, and Latin-Americans in film, and condemns Hollywood for its "thoughtlessness and short-sightedness."

111. Handelman, Janet. "Report on the FLIC-EFLA Minorities Film Workshop." FILM LIBRARY QUARTERLY, 4 (Winter 1970-71): 7-9.

    Concentrates on an analysis of Bert Salzman's GERONIMO JONES with references to BALLAD OF CROWFOOT and YOU ARE ON INDIAN LAND.

112. Harmon, Jim, and Donald F. Glut. THE GREAT MOVIE SERIALS: THEIR SOUND AND FURY. Garden City, NY: Doubleday, 1972.

    Although the book deals with all the serials, it does make references to the portrayals of the Indians in such old favorites as THE MIRACLE RIDER, THE LONE RANGER, and THE LAST OF THE MOHICANS.

113. Harrington, John. "Understanding Hollywood's Indian Rhetoric." CANADIAN REVIEW OF AMERICAN

STUDIES, 8 (Spring 1977): 77-88.

Analyzes the psychology of the Indian image in film and particularly focuses on LITTLE BIG MAN, ULZANA'S RAID, and WHEN THE LEGENDS DIE.

114. Harris, Helen L. "The Bi-Centennial Celebration." INDIAN HISTORIAN, 7 (Fall 1974): 5-8.

    Uses THE READER'S DIGEST film TOM SAWYER which portrays an uncivilized Injun Joe with an obsession for revenge as an example of a misinterpretation of Mark Twain, as well as American history.

115. Harrison, Louis Reeves. "The 'Bison-101' Headliners." MOVING PICTURE WORLD, 12 (April 27, 1912): 320-322.

    Praises the reality and accuracy of a recent spate of films on the "struggles between the primitive red man and the all-conquering white race." He describes the Indians as scattered over what is now the United States "subject to the ravages of relentless killing and torture--cruel, crafty, and predatory--with no universal language, no marks of gradual enlightenment and incapable of contributing anything of value to human evolution" when the Europeans arrived. Constantly exposed by their peaceful occupations to the indiscriminate slaughter by the Indians, these Europeans, nevertheless, subdued them and now provide for their well-being in a manner still "unenjoyed by white citizens."

116. Hartman, Hedy. "A Brief Review of the Native American in American Cinema." INDIAN HISTORIAN, 9 (Summer 1976): 27-29.

    Includes the American Indian Movement's list of

criticisms about Indian portrayal in Hollywood movies as well as comments about some of the best (NANOOK OF THE NORTH) and the worst (NORTHWEST PASSAGE) of the films made with Indian content.

117. Henderson, Robert M. D.W. GRIFFITH: THE YEARS AT BIOGRAPH. New York: Farrar, Straus, and Giroux, 1970.

    Brief discussion of Griffith's Indian films and a listing of one and two reel films with Indian subjects.

118. Hill, Richard. "'In Our Own Image': Review of Current Native American Films." TURTLE, 3 (Summer 1981): 4-5.

    Excerpts from reviews of BROKEN ARROW, CHEYENNE AUTUMN, HOUSE MADE OF DAWN, LITTLE BIG MAN, WINDWALKER, and THE WHITE DAWN.

119. Hutton, Paul A. "The Celluloid Custer." RED RIVER VALLEY HISTORICAL REVIEW, 4 (Fall 1979): 20-43.

    Traces the image of Custer in films from Selig's 1909 one-reeler to LITTLE BIG MAN in 1970. Forty films are discussed in terms which Hutton calls "a flexible myth that changed in response to changing social values."

120. Jacobs, Tom. "Indian Image Debunked." ALBUQUERQUE JOURNAL, Feb. 15, 1982, p. 1B.

    Summary of an Indian film conference at the University of New Mexico with comments from Indian filmmaker Phil Lucas and actors Robert Redford and Geraldine Keams.

121. Jones, Daryl. THE DIME NOVEL WESTERN. Bowling Green, OH: Bowling Green Popular Press, 1978.

    This analysis of the dime novel outlines the characteristics in the genre--structure, plot, and the unifying vision.

122. Jones, Daryl E. "The Earliest Western Films." JOURNAL OF POPULAR FILM AND TELEVISION, 8 (1980): 42-46.

    Surveys the films that led up to the development of the Western genre and concludes that THE GREAT TRAIN ROBBERY was the first film to contain all the essential elements of a Western.

123. Kaufmann, Donald L. "The Indian as Media Hand-Me-Down." COLORADO QUARTERLY, 23 (Spring 1974): 489-504.

    Traces the use of the Indian figure in colonial literature (drama and novels) through the dime novel and the Wild West shows into the movies. He views Indians as a "figment of history always in the making and never coming to an ethnic rest."

124. Kendall, Martha. "Forget the Masked Man. Who Was His Indian Companion?" SMITHSONIAN, 8 (Sept. 1977): 113-120.

    Attempts to linguistically analyze "Kemo sabe" and concludes that, although many possibilities exist, Tonto and the Lone Ranger are mythic characters and cannot be fixed in historical reality.

125. Kennedy, Burt. "Our Way West: Burt Kennedy talks to John Ford." FILMS AND FILMING, 16 (1969): 30-32.

In this interview John Ford discusses the use of Monument Valley as a film location and his preference for black and white photography.

126. Keshena, Rita. "The Role of American Indians in Motion Pictures." AMERICAN INDIAN CULTURE AND RESEARCH JOURNAL, 1 (1974): 25-28.

    Reviews profit-making and exploitation of the American Indian by the motion picture industry.

127. Kitchin, Laurence. "Decline of the Western." LISTENER, 76 (July 14, 1966): 54-57.

    Discusses the Western as "fifty years of mostly stereotyped fantasy." There are brief comments on Ford's CHEYENNE AUTUMN.

128. Kitses, Jim. HORIZONS WEST: STUDIES IN AUTHORSHIP IN THE WESTERN FILM. Bloomington: Indiana University Press, 1970.

    Provides only minor references to the Indian with two exceptions: a brief mention of Sam Peckinpah's handling of the Apaches in MAJOR DUNDEE and some sketchy discussion of the role of the Indian in the Westerns of Anthony Mann.

129. Lacey, Richard. "Alternatives to Cinema Rouge." MEDIA AND METHODS, 7 (April 1971): 70-71.

    Discusses some of the films that the author believes have portrayed Indian people accurately: THE EXILES, TWO RODE TOGETHER, and THE OUTSIDER.

130. Larkins, Robert. "Hollywood and the Indian." FOCUS ON FILM, No. 2 (March-April 1970): 44-53.

Reviews several films with Indian plots that were produced since 1950, concentrating especially on Ford's Westerns.

131. LaRoque, Emma. "And Now a Movie: and TOM SAWYER Criticized." WASSAJA, 2 (March-April 1974): 14.

    A criticism of THE READER'S DIGEST production of TOM SAWYER, attacking especially the inaccurate portrayal of Injun Joe and the unnecessary emphasis on that character.

132. Laughlin, Tom, and Beverly Walker. "Billy Jack vs. Hollywood." FILM COMMENT, 13 (July-August 1977): 24-30.

    Interview with Laughlin introduced by background on the films he has written and directed as well as insights into Laughlin's personality and legal battles.

133. Lichtenstein, Grace. "He Refuses to be an 'Ugh-Tonto' Indian." NEW YORK TIMES, June 6, 1976, p. 13.

    An insightful look at the life of Will Sampson, Creek painter and actor who had his first part as Chief Bromden in ONE FLEW OVER THE CUCKOO'S NEST.

134. Lichtenstein, Grace. "What Made Hollywood Hop Back in the Saddle Again." NEW YORK TIMES, May 16, 1976, p. II, 1.

    An article on Hollywood's apparent renewed interest in Westerns, noting recent films such as RETURN OF A MAN CALLED HORSE.

135. Livingston, Richard O. "Carol Burnett Show

Degrades the American Indian." INDIAN HISTORIAN, 6 (Spring 1973): 23.

In a long letter to the editor, Livingston protests the degrading portrayal of American Indians on a Carol Burnett Show segment in which religious ceremonies were turned into comedy routines.

136. McClure, Arthur F., and Ken D. Jones. HEROES, HEAVIES AND SAGEBRUSH: A PICTORIAL HISTORY OF THE "B" WESTERN PLAYERS. New York: A.S. Barnes and Company, 1972.

Contains an entire chapter on Indian actors who played in the "B" westerns with a photo and brief biographical listing for each of them.

137. Manchell, Frank. CAMERAS WEST. Englewood Cliffs, NJ: Prentice-Hall, Inc., 1971.

This brief historical study of the Western contains scattered references to the treatment of American Indians in American films.

138. Mantell, Harold. "Counteracting the Stereotype." AMERICAN INDIAN, 5 (Fall 1950): 16-20.

This report of the National Film Committee of the Association of American Indian Affairs cites the Committee's input on BROKEN ARROW as an example of how American Indian consultants can change the Hollywood image.

139. Marsden, Michael T., and Jack Nachbar. "The Buried Hatchet: Indian Culture in Film as Victim of the Popular Tradition" in HANDBOOK OF NORTH AMERICAN INDIANS. Vol. 7. Washington, DC: The Smithsonian Institution, 1977.

Discusses the changing Indian image in film as
reflections of political and social periods of the
20th century.

140. May, Jill P. "Native Americans in Media: Using
Valuable Material Concerning Indians." SHANTIH,
4 (Summer-Fall 1979): 60-64.

Discusses and evaluates a number of films and
filmstrips, mostly documentaries.

141. Maynard, Richard A. THE AMERICAN WEST ON FILM:
MYTH AND REALITY. Rochelle Park, NY: Hayden
Book Company, 1975.

This collection of previously published articles,
publicity blurbs, and movie reviews contains an
excerpt from an essay by Vine Deloria, Jr., "The
Problem of Indian Leadership," some publicity
material, and two reviews of the film GERONIMO.

142. Metoyer-Duran, Cheryl. "Media Stereotyping of
American Indians: An Editorial Focus."
AMERICAN INDIAN LIBRARIES NEWSLETTER, 3 (Fall
1978): 1-2.

Focuses on stereotyping on television and the
issues to be dealt with if the negative representation of American Indians is to be changed.

143. Miller, Don. "New Words on Old Westerns." FOCUS
ON FILM, 11 (Autumn 1972): 27-37.

Includes brief studies of several Westerns
including DEVIL'S DOORWAY (1950), a film in which
Indians figure prominently.

144. Millstead, Thomas. "The Movie the Indians Almost

Won." WESTWAYS, 62 (Dec. 1970): 24-26, 55.

Although the author suffers from his own biases, this article is an interesting account of the 1913 filming of a movie with Buffalo Bill and the Sioux of South Dakota. The movie was to be a reenactment of the Battle of Wounded Knee and the strained relations between the Indians and the cavalry brought in to participate almost made filming impossible.

145. Mitchell, George. "Thomas H. Ince." FILMS IN REVIEW, 11 (Oct. 1960): 464-484.

    Biography which makes reference to CUSTER'S LAST FIGHT and the use of Sioux Indians in that movie.

146. Morgenstern, Joseph. "Requiem for a Red Man." NEWSWEEK, 74 (Dec. 8, 1969): 121.

    The writer-director Abraham Polonsky of TELL THEM WILLIE BOY IS HERE is in search of a "pattern of white America's attitude toward non-white minorities."

147. Nachbar, Jack. FOCUS ON THE WESTERN. Englewood Cliffs, NJ: Prentice-Hall, Inc., 1974.

    Includes some articles that refer to the image of the American Indian in Hollywood Westerns. Katherine Esselman's article is especially good in that it traces the Indian image from early writings to the visual media.

148. Nachbar, Jack. "Seventy Years on the Trail: A Selected Chronology of the Western Movie." JOURNAL OF POPULAR FILM, 2 (Winter 1973): 75-83.

A chronology of Westerns which includes brief mention of the various important films about Native Americans.

149. Nachbar, John G. WESTERN FILMS: AN ANNOTATED CRITICAL BIBLIOGRAPHY. New York: Garland Publishing Company, 1975.

    Contains scattered references to articles on films dealing with Indians in the Western.

150. Niver, Kent R., compiler. BIOGRAPH BULLETINS: 1896-1908. Los Angeles: Locare Research Group, 1971.

    Collection of Biograph ads for films. Many of the early films featured American Indian performers and subject matter.

151. O'Connor, John E. THE HOLLYWOOD INDIAN: STEREOTYPES OF NATIVE AMERICANS IN FILMS. Trenton, NJ: State Museum, 1980.

    General discussion of stereotypes with specific essays on AMERICA (1924), THE VANISHING AMERICAN (1926), MASSACRE (1934), DRUMS ALONG THE MOHAWK (1939), THEY DIED WITH THEIR BOOTS ON (1941), DEVIL'S DOORWAY (1949), BROKEN ARROW (1950), CHEYENNE AUTUMN (1964), TELL THEM WILLIE BOY IS HERE (1969), and LITTLE BIG MAN (1970).

152. O'Connor, John E., and Martin A. Jackson. AMERICAN HISTORY/AMERICAN FILM: INTERPRETING THE HOLLYWOOD IMAGE. New York: Frederick Unger Publishing Co., 1979.

    Includes O'Connor's essay on DRUMS ALONG THE MOHAWK in which he compares the novel and the film and the portrayal on screen of agrarian

ARTICLES AND BOOKS

American life "menaced by barbarous Indians."

153. Oman, Mary M. "They Shoot Indians, Don't They?" CINEMA CANADA, 19 (May and June 1975): 11.

Reviews the work of Access, an Alberta film company making educational films. She briefly discusses TAILFEATHERS and NATIVE SCHOOLING.

154. Pauly, Thomas H. "What's Happened to the Western Movie?" WESTERN HUMANITIES REVIEW, 28 (Summer 1974): 260-269.

Comments on the reversals in Westerns, one of which is that the Indian (rather than the cowboy) has become the hero. LITTLE BIG MAN (1970), according to the author, proved that the "Indian's main strength lay in being the tragic victims of the white man's demented thirst for land and gold and glory."

155. Pilkington, William T., and Don Graham. WESTERN MOVIES. Albuquerque: University of New Mexico Press, 1979.

A few individual essays included in this volume contain a discussion of the Indian in the film, most notably the essay on FORT APACHE in which the author describes the inherent respect between white and Indian and discusses Ford's point of view that the Indian had a legitimate complaint against white society. Includes Jack Nachbar on ULZANA'S RAID, Dan Georgakas on A MAN CALLED HORSE, and John Turner on LITTLE BIG MAN.

156. Place, J.A. THE WESTERN FILMS OF JOHN FORD. Secaucus, NJ: The Citadel Press, 1973.

In this excellent study of John Ford's Westerns,

Place provides ample discussion of those films of Ford which dealt with Native Americans. Includes a brief plot summary, some stills, plus a brief analysis of each film. This volume provides an accessible way to examine Ford's use of the Indian in his Westerns.

157. Price, John A. "The Stereotyping of North American Indians in Motion Pictures." ETHNO-HISTORY, 20 (Spring 1973): 153-171.

 Traces the images of Indians from the silent film period (1908-1929) through the negative images of the serials (1930-1947) and the breaking down of stereotypes after 1948. It also discusses the more positive treatment of the Eskimos in documentary movies.

158. Rarihokwats. "THE ONLY GOOD INDIAN. . .: THE HOLLYWOOD GOSPEL." AKWESASNE NOTES, 5 (Late Summer 1973): 41.

 The editor of this Indian newspaper comments about the treatment of the Indian in the movies and praises the Friars' book which examines the topic.

159. Rice, Susan. ". . . And Afterwards, Take Him To a Movie." MEDIA AND METHODS, 7 (April 1971): 43-44, 71-72.

 Contains a broad survey of the current revisionist films about Indians including LITTLE BIG MAN, TELL THEM WILLIE BOY IS HERE, SOLDIER BLUE, FLAP, and THE OUTSIDER which she finds variously mindless, embarrassing, and inadequate. She wonders if the first really intelligent film about Indians might not be made by a foreigner.

ARTICLES AND BOOKS

160. Richburg, James R., and Phyllis R. Hastings. "Media and the American Indian: Ethnographical, Historical, and Contemporary Issues." SOCIAL EDUCATION, 36 (May 1972): 526-533, 562.

Discusses the use of visual materials to teach about the American Indian and reviews several suitable films.

161. Rieupeyrout, Jean-Louis. "The Western: A Historical Genre." QUARTERLY REVIEW OF FILM, RADIO AND TELEVISION, 7 (Winter 1952): 116-128.

Examines two John Ford classics, MY DARLING CLEMENTINE and FORT APACHE, from the perspective of the Western as a historical genre which is a "crystallizer" of diffuse elements from American folklore. In looking at FORT APACHE, the author points out how Ford used the Custer legend in his story of Colonel Thursday's dedication to duty and the destruction of the Indian. The film is touted as an example of the Western epic in its purest form, i.e., purely factual.

162. Robb, David. "Minorities' Minority PIC-TV Roles." VARIETY, 199 (April 4, 1983): 1, 14.

This review of the Screen Actors' Guild survey, "Minority Casting Summary Report," presents current statistics on minority representation in motion pictures and television. The report covers July, 1981, through September, 1982. In answering why there is such a low representation of minorities, Robb says the prevailing reason is "a form of de facto discrimination."

163. Rothel, David. WHO WAS THAT MASKED MAN? THE STORY OF THE LONE RANGER. New York: A.S. Barnes and Co., 1976.

Traces the history of the creation of the Lone Ranger and his subsequent career in print, on radio and television, and in motion pictures. It also contains information on Tonto, his creation, the actors who have played him, and the evolution of his character.

164. Rothwell, Stephen J., ed. FILMS ON INDIANS AND INUIT OF NORTH AMERICA, 1965-1978. Ottawa, Canada: Ministry of Indian and Northern Affairs, 1978.

    A filmography of documentaries which is annotated in both English and French.

165. Rowland, Roy. "The Western as History." FILMS IN REVIEW, 3 (May 1952): 220-234.

    Argues that the Western legend is often more powerful than fact and cites the various disputes over the Battle of Little Big Horn as an example of the kind of historical bog filmmakers can get stuck in if they try to portray what "actually" happened.

166. Schmitz, Tony. "Film Makers' Reflections on the Productions of the American Indian Artists Series." ARIZONA HIGHWAYS, 52 (August 1976): 4-11.

    Discusses the making of the American Indian Artists Film Series which depicted the working of American Indian artists for KAET, a public television station in Phoenix, Arizona.

167. Silet, Charles L.P. "American Indian Images: A Review Essay." NAIES NEWSLETTER, 7 (Oct. 1982): 38-44.

ARTICLES AND BOOKS

Reviews SAVAGISM AND CIVILITY: INDIANS AND ENGLISHMEN IN COLONIAL VIRGINIA; THE HALF-BLOOD: A CULTURAL SYMBOL IN 19TH CENTURY AMERICAN FICTION; and FACING WEST: THE METAPHYSICS OF INDIAN-HATING AND EMPIRE BUILDING. He also reviews the classic accounts of Indian-white relationships which deal with the place of the American Indian in American history and culture.

168. Silet, Charles L.P. "The Image of the American Indian in Film" in THE WORLDS BETWEEN TWO RIVERS; PERSPECTIVES ON AMERICAN INDIANS IN IOWA. Eds. Gretchen Bataille, David M. Gradwohl, and Charles L.P. Silet. Ames: Iowa State University Press, 1978. Pp. 10-15.

    Surveys the sources for film stereotypes and how such stereotypes have been perpetuated in the 20th century.

169. Silet, Charles L.P., and Gretchen M. Bataille. "The Indian in the Film: A Critical Survey." QUARTERLY REVIEW OF FILM STUDIES, 2 (Feb. 1977): 56-74.

    Reviews popular images of the American Indian as they have influenced films and film criticism. Includes material from early in the twentieth century up to contemporary reviews.

170. Sinclair, Andrew. JOHN FORD. New York: The Dial Press, 1979.

    Includes a discussion of CHEYENNE AUTUMN and points out the compromises made during production. This biography contains material about Ford's earlier films which involved American Indian subject matter.

171. Smith, James R. "Native American Images and the Broadcast Media." AMERICAN INDIAN CULTURE AND RESEARCH JOURNAL, 5 (1981): 81-92.

    Evaluates radio and television and compares the treatment of the American Indian with the film treatment. He speculates that the future is unclear; film could aid in the improvement of the Indian image or could further denigrate the Indian position.

172. Spears, Jack. HOLLYWOOD: THE GOLDEN ERA. New York: A.S. Barnes, 1971.

    Acknowledges that Hollywood has had little concern for historical accuracy or honest characterization and illustrates with comments the portrayal of the Indian on the screen.

173. Spears, Jack. "The Indian on the Screen." FILMS IN REVIEW, 10 (Jan. 1959): 18-35.

    Discusses the stereotyped Indian villain and the noble savage as well as the oversympathetic portrayals of American Indians in films since 1950.

174. Spenser, Richard V. "Los Angeles Notes: Indians Protest Against Indian Pictures." MOVING PICTURE WORLD, 8 (March 18, 1911): 587.

    Indians of Northwest and Western reservations were registering objections with the Bureau of Indian Affairs against portrayals of Indian life in films. The commissioner, Robert G. Valentine, said he was also disturbed and would help the Shoshone, Cheyenne, and Arapahoe delegates to eliminate the objectionable portrayals.

175. Stabiner, Karen. "Experts for Hire: Authenticity Hollywood Style." NEW YORK TIMES, Dec. 31, 1978, p. 13D.

   Two film advisers, Rabbi Steven Robbins and George American Horse, comment on their influence, or lack of it, on Hollywood productions.

176. Steiner, Stan. "Real Horses and Mythic Riders." AMERICAN WEST, 18 (Sept.-Oct. 1981): 54-59.

   Reports on the Western Film Festival in Santa Fe in 1981. Iron Eyes Cody recollects that there may have been ten movies NOT insulting to Indians.

177. Talbot, Anne. "Prejudice: Thoughts Garnered Among the Navajo." MEDIA AND METHODS, 9 (Dec. 1972): 36-37.

   Lists three films about American Indians and discusses the prejudice held against the Navajos by teachers.

178. Terraine, John. "End of the Trail." FILMS AND FILMING, 3 (July 1957): 9, 30.

   Argues that the American Indian was never much of a "noble savage." "He was brave and intelligent, cruel and smelly, and he had no drawingroom manners at all."

179. Tuska, Jon. THE FILMING OF THE WEST. New York: Doubleday and Co., 1976.

   This history of the Western contains a number of chapters or portions of chapters devoted to discussing the role of the Native American in the genre. Particularly notable are the sections on THE SQUAW MAN, THE INDIANS ARE COMING, FORT APACHE, SHE WORE

A YELLOW RIBBON, BROKEN ARROW, RUN OF THE ARROW, HONDO, and MCLINTOCK.

180. U.S. Commission on Civil Rights. WINDOW DRESSING ON THE SET: WOMEN AND MINORITIES IN TELEVISION. Washington, DC: USGPO, 1977.

    Study of the portrayal of minorities and women in television drama, news, and employment at the networks.

181. U.S. Commission on Civil Rights. WINDOW DRESSING ON THE SET: AN UPDATE. Washington, DC: USGPO, 1979.

    Updates previous report by covering years 1975-1977 with an emphasis on television's treatment of women and minorities.

182. Vestal, Stanley. "The Hollywooden Indian." SOUTHWEST REVIEW, 21 (1936): 418-423.

    Criticizes the movie portrayal of Indian people as "caricatures of their race" and blames directors for not using Indian actors.

183. Vickrey, William. "Some Wrongs Righted on Film: The Vanishing American: Part II." FILM LIBRARY QUARTERLY, 3 (Winter 1969-1970): 46-47.

    Reviews ISHI IN TWO WORLDS, TAHTONKA, and CIRCLE OF THE SUN.

184. Wagenknecht, Edward. "Griffith's Biographs." FILMS IN REVIEW, 26 (Oct. 1975): 449-467.

    In this bibliographical essay on Griffith's films, Wagenknecht says Griffith used American

Indians as his principal minority group and the treatment was consistently sympathetic even if sometimes inauthentic.

185. Walker, Stanley. "Let the Indian Be the Hero." NEW YORK TIMES MAGAZINE, April 24, 1960, pp. VI, 50, 52, 55.

    General discussion of the Indian in television Westerns and a plea that perhaps someday the Indian will be the hero rather than the victim of inaccurate portrayals.

186. Weatherford, Elizabeth. NATIVE AMERICANS ON FILM AND VIDEO. New York: Museum of the American Indian, 1981.

    Lists 400 documentary films and videotapes, many made by American Indians and portraying ethnographic details. Some fictional material is included, but those films portray American Indian culture and perspectives accurately. The resource section includes addresses of media centers and information on film conferences.

187. Wilkinson, Gerald. "Colonialism through the Media." INDIAN HISTORIAN, 7 (Summer 1974): 29-32.

    Points out that the media paints a picture of Indian people that serves the interest of the white public and not necessarily truth or justice. A subtle and pervasive control of Indians' psychology, their image of themselves, their values, and their culture is possible through the stereotypic portrait drawn by the media. The author argues for more Indian participation in ownership and control of media.

188. Willett, Ralph. "The American Western: Myth and Anti-myth." JOURNAL OF POPULAR CULTURE, 4 (Fall 1970): 455-463.

   Argues that the pre-fifties stereotyping of the Native American is now well recognized.

189. Woll, Allen. THE LATIN AMERICAN IMAGE IN AMERICAN FILM. Los Angeles: UCLA Latin American Series, 1980.

   Includes brief mention of Incan and Aztec portrayal on film.

190. Wood, Michael. "Hi Ho, Silver!" NEW YORK REVIEW OF BOOKS, 23 (July 15, 1976): 29-30.

   Reviews the book SIX GUNS AND SOCIETY by Will Wright and the films THE MISSOURI BREAKS and BUFFALO BILL AND THE INDIANS. Wood sees the films as attempts to revise the myth of the West, a myth of the frontier that has become true for many Americans.

191. Wood, Robin. "Shall We Gather At the River: The Late Films of John Ford." FILM COMMENT, 7 (Fall 1971): 8-17.

   Criticizes Ford's ability to create a really convincing view of the Cheyenne which resulted in the artistic failure of CHEYENNE AUTUMN. His self-contradiction in dealing with Indians flaws the film. The article also deals in a general way with Ford's treatment of Indians in SHE WORE A YELLOW RIBBON and FORT APACHE.

192. Worth, Sol, and John Adair. THROUGH NAVAJO EYES: AN EXPLORATION IN FILM COMMUNICATION AND ANTHROPOLOGY. Bloomington: Indiana University

Press, 1972.

Documents the experiences of the authors as they taught the Navajo to make films and describes the results that illustrated in part how a given culture structures reality.

193. Wright, Will. SIX GUNS AND SOCIETY: A STRUCTURAL STUDY OF THE WESTERN. Berkeley: University of California Press, 1975.

    This sociological study of the Western contains only brief mention of the role of the Native American in the myth of the West.

194. Yacowar, Maurice. "Aspects of the Familiar: A Defense of Minority Group Stereotyping in the Popular Film." LITERATURE/FILM QUARTERLY, 2 (Spring 1974): 129-139.

    Discusses stereotyping as part of film formula--a kind of iconography that says more about white society than the minorities who are stereotyped. He views the stereotyped blacks, Indians, women, and Jews as metaphors.

Reviews of Individual Films

Reviews of Individual Films

195. "American Legends." VOGUE, 166 (June 1976): 116-117.

In this review of Altman's BUFFALO BILL AND THE INDIANS no mention is made of the roles of Indians in the film.

196. "And Another Redskin. . . ." NEWSWEEK, 31 (May 17, 1948): 95.

The author refers to Indians being on the warpath and paints a picture of an old Indian fighter. The reviewer concludes that FORT APACHE succeeds in "bringing back the time-honored business of making Redskins bite the dust as first-rate entertainment."

197. "Big Jack for Billy Jack." NEWSWEEK, 81 (March 26, 1973): 72.

Discusses the legal battles between Tom Laughlin and Warner Brothers on the distribution of BILLY JACK.

198. [Review of BROKEN ARROW]. CHRISTIAN CENTURY, 67 (Sept. 13, 1950): 1087.

Sees the Indians as being portrayed as

individuals "with culture and codes to be respected," and admits the presence of evil on both sides.

199. [Review of BROKEN ARROW]. NEWSWEEK, 36 (August 7, 1950): 76.

   In a summary of the film, the reviewer analyzes the film as ending when "Cochise turns out to be a right guy who realizes the futility of warring against the white man."

200. [Review of BROKEN ARROW]. TIME, 56 (July 31, 1950): 62.

   The film reflects a change in the portrayal: "Instead of blood-lusting savages who whoop endlessly across the U.S. screen, its Indians are proud, dignified warriors with their own cultural tradition, a stern code of honor, and a justified hatred of the white invaders."

201. [Review of BUFFALO BILL]. LIFE, 16 (April 10, 1944): 109-117.

   Calls Buffalo Bill a "rugged symbol of the faraway age when buffalo roamed the range, scouts led U.S. cavalry to the rescue, and the only good Indian was a dead Indian."

202. [Review of CHEYENNE AUTUMN]. AMERICA, 112 (Jan. 16, 1965): 85.

   Although Ford wishes to tell the story from the Indian's point of view, "the Cheyennes never emerge as much more than long-suffering puppets."

203. "Entertainment." NEWSWEEK, 15 (Feb. 26, 1940): 29.

NORTHWEST PASSAGE is described as an exciting and suspenseful film that is close to a documentary account of the attack and merciless slaughter of the Abenaki Indians.

204. "The Exiles." TIME, 94 (Dec. 19, 1969): 76-77.

    Praises Abraham Polonsky for his "hard, gritty" portrayal of racial persecution in TELL THEM WILLIE BOY IS HERE.

205. "Fallen Angel on Location." TIME, 95 (Feb. 2, 1970): 71.

    In this review of SOLDIER BLUE, the reviewer concentrates on star Candace Bergen who says she wanted to do the film because it was the "first script I have read where the Indian was not saying 'How' and running around committing atrocities."

206. "Following the Films." SCHOLASTIC, 36 (Feb. 26, 1940): 36.

    Describes the actions of Roger's Rangers in NORTHWEST PASSAGE as courageous and daring against savage Indians who had terrorized New England villagers.

207. "Hollywood Angles re BUFFALO BILL." VARIETY, 283 (July 7, 1976): 28.

    Twenty minutes were cut from BUFFALO BILL AND THE INDIANS for the European market and the reviewer discusses the implications of the cut.

208. "Home of the Braves." TIME, 95 (May 11, 1970): 103.

Believes that director Elliott Silverstein "capitalizes on honesty" in his portrayal of the Indians in A MAN CALLED HORSE.

209. "Indian Exodus." TIME, 85 (Jan. 8, 1965): 54.

This review of CHEYENNE AUTUMN discusses the historical episode on which the movie is based, stating that it was "bleak" for the Cheyenne Indians and that the movie's strongest scenes touch on the senseless murder of the Indians.

210. "Kalem Indian Stories Popular." MOVING PICTURE WORLD, 6 (June 25, 1910): 1099.

Lauds Kalem directors for their background knowledge and the authenticity displayed in their Indian films. The article predicts that an upcoming film, CHEYENNE RAIDERS, will be as popular as previous ones because of such thrills as real leaps to death over real precipices into unseen nets below.

211. [Review of A MAN CALLED HORSE]. AMERICA, 122 (May 16, 1970): 538.

Describes the film as dramatizing the present conditions of American Indians by portraying the past culture with dignity and integrity.

212. [Review of MASSACRE]. NEWSWEEK IN ENTERTAINMENT, 3 (Jan. 27, 1934): 33.

Finds this melodrama hard to believe at times: "If half the white man's abuses of Indians shown in this First National film are true, it is a wonder any Redskins have survived at all."

REVIEWS

213. "More Loathsome Films." AMERICA, 123 (Sept. 19, 1970): 185-186.

SOLDIER BLUE fails to portray the Indians as three-dimensional figures. Nelson is criticized for taking an incident out of context and falsifying details to present a general indictment of white treatment of American Indians.

214. "Movies." NEWSWEEK, 18 (Dec. 1, 1941): 70.

THEY DIED WITH THEIR BOOTS ON is described as a cross between a Western and an epic. The major problem is that it takes too long to get to the Indians. Custer is seen as a victim of bad luck and bad judgment.

215. "Noble Non-savage: Chief Dan George." TIME, 97 (Feb. 15, 1971): 76.

Biographical note on Chief Dan George, a comment on his role in LITTLE BIG MAN, and a few words about his philosophy on Indian-white relations.

216. [Review of NORTHWEST MOUNTED POLICE]. TIME, 36 (Nov. 11, 1940): 74.

Claims the movie has an "earnest devotion to accuracy" and refers to the "ruthless attack of Indians and half-breeds."

217. [Review of NORTHWEST PASSAGE]. LIFE, 8 (March 18, 1940): 50-51.

A brief review which has a general tone of Indians as "bad guys." Indians are described as "blood thirsty," "fierce," and "drunken."

218. "THE PLAINSMAN." NEWSWEEK, 9 (Jan. 16, 1937): 30.

   Little mention is made of Indians being in the film, and the focus is on the glory of those who beat the redskin. Comments that "real" Indians were used in the film as though it were a completely new idea.

219. [Review of RAMONA]. TIME, 28 (Oct. 5, 1936): 28.

   Emphasizes the "traditional white methods of dealing with Indians, civilized or raw."

220. [Review of SAVAGE INNOCENTS]. MCCALL'S, 88 (Dec. 1960): 180.

   A fairly well-balanced review which cites specifics of Eskimo culture and looks at the movie from two points of view.

221. "THEY DIED WITH THEIR BOOTS ON." TIME, 38 (Dec. 22, 1941): 47.

   This first full-length exposition of the Custer legend whitewashes Custer and bypasses history in a way not likely to please either side.

222. [Review of WALK THE PROUD LAND]. TIME, 68 (Sept. 24, 1956): 92-94.

   The Indians in the film are "good guys" and the film portrays the Apaches as human.

223. [Review of WHEN THE LEGENDS DIE]. TIME, 100 (Nov. 6, 1972): 86.

   A positive review of a film which "genuinely

seems to express, even in a small way, the strangled rage and uncertainty of the modern Indian."

224. "THE WHITE BUFFALO." VARIETY, 282 (April 28, 1976): 3.

   Discusses technical problems with the film episodes and settings, particularly the snow and avalanche scenes.

225. Agabiti, Thomas. "Samuel Fuller's RUN OF THE ARROW and the Mythos of Romance: An Archetypal Analysis." FILM READER, 2 (1977): 96-110.

   Applies archetypal criticism to film using RUN OF THE ARROW as an example.

226. Alexander, Shana. "The Sad Lot of the Sioux." LIFE, 66 (Feb. 7, 1969): 14E.

   Reactions to the filming of A MAN CALLED HORSE and Alexander's views of the Sioux people who acted in the film.

227. Allen, T. "A Summer Tonic of Humor." AMERICA, 135 (Sept. 4, 1976): 99-100.

   Allen makes only brief mention of BUFFALO BILL AND THE INDIANS and makes no mention of the Indians in the film.

228. Astor, Gerald. "Good Guys Wear War Paint." LOOK, 34 (Dec. 1, 1970): 56-61.

   Interviews with Dustin Hoffman and Richard Mulligan about their roles in LITTLE BIG MAN with comments from Arthur Penn. This article describes the film experience as "the losing of the west."

229. Bell, Arthur. "Neigh." COMMONWEAL, 92 (June 26, 1970): 318.

Criticizes the confused standards Hollywood exhibits toward the Indian in films which are present in A MAN CALLED HORSE. He quotes a press release describing the film as not just another "Hollywood version of the Indian legend but the Indian's own statement of their trials."

230. Berstein, Gene M. "Robert Altman's BUFFALO BILL AND THE INDIANS OR SITTING BULL'S HISTORY LESSON: A Self-Portrait in Celluloid." JOURNAL OF POPULAR CULTURE, 13 (Summer 1979): 17-25.

Discusses the film as "reflexive," about the film medium, the Western, and the creation of a super-star (Buffalo Bill). The two titles reflect a dual view of history--Buffalo Bill's and Sitting Bull's.

231. Boyd, George N. "From a Comfortable Distance." CHRISTIAN CENTURY, 88 (Oct. 13, 1971): 1213-1214.

The film BILLY JACK relies on stereotypes, the romance of the first American, and the questionable heroics of Billy Jack, the "half-breed ex-Green Beret war hero and karate expert." Trying to have it all ways, the film fails to be convincing."

232. Braudy, Leo. "Difficulties of LITTLE BIG MAN." FILM QUARTERLY, 25 (Fall 1971): 30-33.

Focuses on the character of Jack Crabb and

discusses the film as the embodiment of a sense of loss of time, of youth, and of opportunity.

233. Browne, Nicholas. "The Spectator-in-the-Text: The Rhetoric of STAGECOACH." FILM QUARTERLY, 29 (1976): 26-38.

 In a discussion of the classical narrative film, Browne examines the connection between the act of narration and the imagery in STAGECOACH.

234. Brudnoy, David. "Film Chronicle: Hoffman, Jagger and That's It." NATIONAL REVIEW, 23 (April 6, 1971): 381.

 Describes LITTLE BIG MAN as embodying and scorning the old myths of the West, playing the cliches (noble savage, savage redskin, civilized white, brutal racist, and so on) against each other.

235. Bryon, Stuart. "A Vision of American Multiplicity." VILLAGE VOICE, 16 (August 19, 1971): 47.

 Discovers in BILLY JACK an attempt to understand and reconcile the two facets of American culture most associated with attitudes toward the Indians: pacificism and violence. He finds the film in the tradition of the modern Western with its use of genre cliches to comment on "historical irony and reality."

236. Buckley, Peter. [Review of SOLDIER BLUE]. FILMS AND FILMING, 17 (June 1971): 65-66.

 Notes that the bloodshed and carnage of this beautifully made film are justified by its moral outrage against the white massacre of Indians.

Buckley found SOLDIER BLUE a powerful and convincing film.

237. Buckley, Tom. "Bad Vibrations." NEW YORK TIMES, April 28, 1978, p. C12.

Describes THE MANITOU as having "an absurd penny-dreadful script and cheap-jack production." The conflict between good and evil Indian spirits is poorly treated.

238. Bucklin, Louise L. [Review of APACHE]. NATIONAL PARENT TEACHER, 48 (June 1954): 38.

APACHE is "a superior western based on a historical episode. . . . His [the Indian] eventual submission is a foregone conclusion, but sympathy and understanding are expressed for his revolt."

239. Budeley, Michael. [Review of MANITOU]. FILMS IN REVIEW, 29 (April 1978): 242.

Describes the film as "so bad it's almost good." The special effects and its potential to be absurdly comic are its only attributes.

240. Burgess, John Andrew. "LITTLE BIG MAN." FILM SOCIETY REVIEW, 6 (March 1971): 30-32.

In a negative review, Burgess says that to have sympathy for the "passing of the Red Man," we must first see the way of life that ended, and Penn fails to show us that. "The movie finally never brings us to know enough about the Indians; when they are slaughtered, we react not to tragedy but to atrocity."

241. Callenbach, Ernest. "Short Notices: THESE ARE MY

PEOPLE and YOU ARE ON INDIAN LAND." FILM QUARTERLY, 24 (Fall 1970): 62.

Reviews THESE ARE MY PEOPLE and YOU ARE ON INDIAN LAND as films which document the process whereby people recognize that their rights have been denied and try to recover them.

242. Canby, Vincent. "HORSE Sequel Retreads Mystic Rite." NEW YORK TIMES, July 29, 1976, p. 19.

Review of THE RETURN OF A MAN CALLED HORSE in which Canby calls Morgan "Billy Jack with an English accent" and the film is depicted as "unpleasantly patronizing."

243. Canby, Vincent. "How the West Was Brutal." NEW YORK TIMES, Dec. 3, 1972, p. II, 1.

In this review of ULZANA'S RAID, Canby says, "The film makes no attempt to justify [Indian] brutality in civilized terms of wrongs done them, nor does it make more than a half-hearted attempt to explain them in their own terms."

244. Canby, Vincent. [Review of A MAN CALLED HORSE]. NEW YORK TIMES, April 30, 1970, p. 46.

Discusses Sioux rituals to some degree and cites the bloodiness as well as what he sees as "emphasis on salvation through mutilation."

245. Canby, Vincent. [Review of WHEN THE LEGENDS DIE]. NEW YORK TIMES, Oct. 20, 1972, p. 37.

Praises WHEN THE LEGENDS DIE as an "intelligent, gentle, almost reticent film" in its depiction of Tom Black Bull.

246. Chavers, Dean. "A Good Movie to Miss." WASSAJA, 4 (Jan. 1976): 20.

   Criticizes WINTERHAWK as a story of "a mysterious savage with a sixth sense." He points out the many technical errors in the film, including a comment about the run in Sasheen Littlefeather's nylons.

247. Clandfield, David. "The Onomastic Code of STAGECOACH." LITERATURE FILM QUARTERLY, 5 (Winter 1977): 174-180.

   Provides a linguistic-structural analysis of character names and place names in STAGECOACH, comparing the names in the Nichol's script with those in the short story by Ernest Haycox.

248. Cocks, Jay. "Indian Giver." TIME, 108 (Sept. 13, 1976): 80.

   THE RETURN OF A MAN CALLED HORSE is called a "silly sequel" to the first film which starred Richard Harris as Sir John Morgan. Cocks compares the movie to "the old Boy Scout ceremony of the Order of the Arrow."

249. Coleman, John. "Bang Bang." NEW STATESMAN, 91 (July 23, 1976): 123-124.

   Brief review of BUFFALO BILL AND THE INDIANS in which he says little about the Indians except to note several ploys that "attribute both greater physical and spiritual powers to the Indians."

250. Coleman, John. "How. Why?" NEW STATESMAN, 92 (Oct. 29, 1976): 609-610.

   Speculates why anyone went to the trouble of

producing THE RETURN OF A MAN CALLED HORSE. The torture scene, being the central scene of the film, is viewed by Coleman as the point at which any "right-minded person ought to start feeling ill."

251. Coleman, John. [Review of MANITOU]. NEW STATESMAN, 97 (May 25, 1979): 765-766.

Calls the film "unpleasant" but praises the "good special effects."

252. Combs, Richard. [Review of MANITOU]. MONTHLY FILM BULLETIN, 45 (Sept. 1978): 177-178.

MANITOU is a demonology film lacking balance dramatically although the special effects are good. It is the story of an evil medicine man who tries to reincarnate himself.

253. Combs, Richard. "ULZANA'S RAID." SIGHT AND SOUND, 42 (Spring 1973): 115-116.

Describes the film as the story of a renegade Apache who rebels against the monotony of the reservation by going on a senseless rampage of rape, torture, and death.

254. Constible, J.P. "WINDWALKER." CINEMA, 75 (July 1981): 34.

Sees the film as more authentic and dignified than most, but believes some of the language is pretentious.

255. Cooper, Arthur. "The Ute and the Brute." NEWSWEEK, 80 (Nov. 6, 1972): 124.

Review of WHEN THE LEGENDS DIE. Cooper says that director Stuart Millar turns the rodeo world into a metaphor for the society that exploited the American Indian. "Millar makes his points about racism and exploitation."

256. Cooper, Arthur. "Wooden Indians." NEWSWEEK, 79 (April 24, 1972): 89-90.

 Criticizes JOURNEY THROUGH ROSEBUD for its attempts to portray a more sensitive view of American Indians and failing. "These sentimentalized Indians seem no more real, arouse little more compassion than the ones who used to bite the dust every Saturday in the B Westerns."

257. Crist, Judith. "The Movies: A Bicentennial Buffalo Bill." SATURDAY REVIEW, 3 (July 19, 1976): 62-63.

 Discusses the creativity of this and other Altman films. Crist describes Sitting Bull as his own person in the film: "he establishes himself, comes and goes as he chooses, defines his own performance."

258. Crist, Judith. "The Movies: Talking About Men, Obsession, and a Clockmaker." SATURDAY REVIEW, 3 (Sept. 18, 1976): 41-42.

 Brief mention of THE RETURN OF A MAN CALLED HORSE.

259. Cunningham, James P. "RAMONA." COMMONWEAL, 25 (Oct. 30, 1936): 20.

 This early review praises the depiction of the injustices inflicted upon the Indians.

260. deMontigny, Lionel H. "A Critique of Film TRIAL OF BILLY JACK." WASSAJA, 3 (Jan.-Feb. 1975): 2.

In this review of the "Indian's answer to Kung Fu," deMontigny describes the film as "the same old stuff about Indians being an 'oppressed minority' and the usual mixture of pagan rituals."

261. Denby, David. "Americana: LITTLE BIG MAN; LOVE STORY." ATLANTIC, 227 (March 1971): 106, 108-109.

Criticizes Penn for impressing certain ideologies of the present onto the past. His portrayal of the Indian is bent on doing two things: "To do away with mumbo jumbo, the ignorant superstition, and the racist fears that have almost always characterized movie portraits of Indians" and "to end the hypocrisy of those liberal Westerns which have shown Indians being betrayed by treacherous whites, only to frighten the audience in the end with the Indians' aroused savagery--which justifies their slaughter."

262. Eder, Richard. "There's a Great Deal More to Acting Than Making Faces." NEW YORK TIMES, August 15, 1976, p. II, 13.

Brief mention of THE RETURN OF A MAN CALLED HORSE.

263. Erens, Patricia. "JEREMIAH JOHNSON: The Mountain Man as Modern Hero." VELVET LIGHT TRAP, 12 (Spring 1974): 37-39.

Discovers in JEREMIAH JOHNSON an interesting reversal of the usual Western prohibition against a white living among the Indians and provides a contemporary, upbeat theme in which the Indian way of life is an important counter-culture symbol.

264. Farber, Stephen. [Review of HOMBRE and WELCOME TO HARD TIMES]. FILM QUARTERLY, 21 (Fall 1967): 49-58.

Describes HOMBRE as not really about racial prejudice, "an overworked subject that doesn't fit easily into the Old West," but uses that prejudice to raise questions about the meaningfulness of participation in a corrupt society.

265. Farber, Stephen. "Short Notices: A MAN CALLED HORSE and FLAP." FILM QUARTERLY, 24 (Fall 1970): 60-61.

A MAN CALLED HORSE is a film with a mixture of terror and wonderment. "From seeing this film, we get some understanding of how New England Puritans must have felt on confronting this savage, foreign people. To superstitious, provincial, unimaginative European settlers, these fierce, bizarrely painted and costumed natives must indeed have looked like monsters from hell."

266. French, Philip. "LITTLE BIG MAN." SIGHT AND SOUND, 40 (Spring 1971): 102-103.

In spite of many fine things, including several parodies of famous Westerns, Penn's film tends to dilute the charge against white America by focusing the guilt for the near genocide of the Indian on one crazy individual, George Armstrong Custer.

267. Gessner, Robert. "The Squaw Man Rides Again." SATURDAY REVIEW OF LITERATURE, 5 (August 1950): 30-31.

Review of BROKEN ARROW which discusses the

involvement of the Association on American Indian Affairs. Gessner remarks, "it's old Indians in a new battle with a square-deal label, it's the best vintage in many a month."

268. Gillett, John. "CHEYENNE AUTUMN." SIGHT AND SOUND, 34 (Winter 1964-1965): 36-37.

    This positive review discusses Ford's increasing disenchantment with "the myths he helped to create," but laments Ford's "division of feeling" toward the significance of his statement about Indians in this film.

269. Gilliatt, Penelope. "The Current Cinema: Back to the Trees." NEW YORKER, 46 (May 9, 1970): 118.

    A MAN CALLED HORSE is a film of Indian life painstakingly well researched: "The torture scenes, for instance, are obviously scholarly in their misbegotten way."

270. Gilliatt, Penelope. "The Current Cinema: The Stronger Sex." NEW YORKER, 52 (August 16, 1976): 82, 85-87.

    Describes THE RETURN OF A MAN CALLED HORSE as "an alarming example of the receding brain" and patronizing toward Indian people.

271. Gilliatt, Penelope. "The Current Cinema: White Dreams." NEW YORKER, 52 (June 28, 1976): 62-63.

    In this review of BUFFALO BILL AND THE INDIANS, Gilliatt discusses what "is fraudulent in the story of white Americans' conquest of a savage land" and the different dreams of Indians and whites.

272. Gow, Gordon. "BUFFALO BILL AND THE INDIANS."
FILMS AND FILMING, 22 (Sept. 1976): 33-34.

Mentions Sitting Bull, "whose glance is sufficient to convey the Indian's proud contempt for the white man who has done wrong under the pretext of doing right."

273. Gow, Gordon. "CHEYENNE AUTUMN." FILMS AND FILMING, 11 (Dec. 1964): 27.

Finds CHEYENNE AUTUMN, perhaps Ford's most profound film, a study of mutual inadequacies in the conflict between whites and Indians in the old West which has been set against the vastness of Monument Valley where men of all colors are dwarfed and need to bid for human dignity.

274. Gow, Gordon. [Review of LITTLE BIG MAN]. FILMS AND FILMING, 17 (June 1971): 63.

Describes LITTLE BIG MAN as endowed with a sophisticated hindsight as it reviews history, sometimes satirically, sometimes seriously, with the seriousness apparently saved for the Indians and Dan George who do much to reverse the Western myth in the movie.

275. Gow, Gordon. [Review of A MAN CALLED HORSE].
FILMS AND FILMING, 17 (Oct. 1970): 45-46.

Sees the film as clouded in part because of the Sioux language dialogue and in part because of the mixture of trappings from both the old and new Westerns.

276. Gow, Gordon. "THE RETURN OF A MAN CALLED HORSE."
FILMS AND FILMING, 23 (Nov. 1976): 29-30.

Compares the sequel to the original A MAN CALLED HORSE, citing the Sun Vow ceremony and bloodletting of the film as more acceptable than it had been in the Silverstein production.

277. Greenspan, Roger. "Candace Bergen Stars in Violent Westerns." NEW YORK TIMES, August 13, 1970, p. 29.

Bemoans the blood, bodies, and destruction of SOLDIER BLUE, giving more credit to the special effects department than the cast or director.

278. Gross, Larry. "Alan Sharp: Screenwriter in a Strange Land." MILLIMETER, 4 (March 1976): 22-25.

Alan Sharp is the author of screenplays for ULZANA'S RAID (1972) and several other Westerns that have been "literate, adult" films.

279. Gustkey, Earl. "Still 'Running Brave.'" SACRAMENTO BEE, 31 July 1983, pp. AA1, 10.

The "real-life" story of Billy Mills is compared to the portrayal in RUNNING BRAVE. Mills calls the film "quality" and reports "I'm very happy with it."

280. Hall, Mordaunt. "VANISHING AMERICAN has Inspiring Scenes." NEW YORK TIMES, Oct. 16, 1925, p. 5.

Comments on Richard Dix and his "impersonation" of a "redskin." Dix apparently had trouble getting his make-up to look right.

281. Handzo, Stephen. "Film: SOLDIER BLUE." VILLAGE

VOICE, 15 (Sept. 10, 1970): 61.

Notes that "during periods of national masochism the Indian is rediscovered." He sees SOLDIER BLUE as a "Theater of Cruelty Western based on proto-My Lai."

282. Handzo, Stephen. "Going through the DEVIL'S DOORWAY: The Early Westerns of Anthony Mann." BRIGHT LIGHTS, 1 (Summer 1976): 4-15.

This lengthy essay on Mann's films places DEVIL'S DOORWAY in the Western genre and discusses in detail the plot, particularly the relationship between Indians and whites in the film.

283. Hartung, Philip T. "The Aim is Peace." COMMONWEAL, 52 (August 4, 1950): 413-414.

Praises BROKEN ARROW as one of the best films to deal with Indian-white relations: "Perhaps BROKEN ARROW oversimplifies the issue but if it succeeds in putting over the argument that in all racial problems there is something to be said for both sides, it deserves big praise." He adds that treating Indians as real people "is a definite step forward in the movies."

284. Hartung, Philip T. [Review of APACHE]. COMMONWEAL, 60 (July 30, 1954): 413.

APACHE highlights the white treatment of Indians by telling the story of Massai, an Indian who refused to give up when Geronimo surrendered in 1886. Hartung calls the white men "the villains of the piece."

285. Hartung, Philip T. "Boys with Whiskers."

COMMONWEAL, 40 (May 5, 1944): 62.

Views BUFFALO BILL as an entertaining film about the West.

286. Hartung, Philip T. [Review of DEVIL'S DOORWAY]. COMMONWEAL, 53 (Nov. 24, 1950): 173.

Finds the film taking the side of the Indians in showing "who settled the land first and who was getting the raw end of the deal."

287. Hartung, Philip T. "Looking, Looking Everywhere." COMMONWEAL, 64 (June 15, 1956): 274.

Describes THE SEARCHERS as thin on plot and compares John Wayne to Captain Ahab, both participating in a relentless and ruthless search.

288. Hartung, Philip T. "Strange Heroes." COMMONWEAL, 35 (Dec. 5, 1941): 180.

Discovers in THEY DIED WITH THEIR BOOTS ON a distortion of history to suit the fancy of scriptwriters. Some of the film is dull and some exciting, but basically the film is too long for its limited content.

289. Hartung, Philip T. [Review of WALK THE PROUD LAND]. COMMONWEAL, 64 (Sept. 7, 1956): 561.

This movie is based on the biography of John Philip Clum, a Bible student who became a government Indian agent in 1874 and frustrated whites by treating the Indians as human beings rather than slaves.

290. Haspiel, James Robert. "THE WHITE BUFFALO."

MONTHLY FILM BULLETIN, 45 (Feb. 1978): 32-33.

Remarks that this film is a Western that could be called "hopeless" or "the worst in years."

291. Hatch, Robert. [Review of BROKEN ARROW]. NEW REPUBLIC, 123 (July 31, 1950): 23.

Sees the Indians portrayed in BROKEN ARROW as "noble as Cato, as long suffering as a Christian martyr." He admits the reversal in the screen image has been long in coming.

292. Hatch, Robert. [Review of BUFFALO BILL AND THE INDIANS]. NATION, 223 (July 31, 1976): 93-94.

BUFFALO BILL AND THE INDIANS makes two basic assertions: the white man gave the red man a dirty deal and the Wild West was a fantasy concocted to conceal how dirty that deal was.

293. Hatch, Robert. [Review of FORT APACHE]. NEW REPUBLIC, 12 (July 1948): 29-30.

Comments that, "The Indians are presented not as heathen devils but as a minority group with a grievance."

294. Hatch, Robert. [Review of THE SEARCHERS]. NATION, 182 (June 23, 1956): 536.

Criticizes the role played by John Wayne, particularly when he shoots an already dead Indian: "This is carrying prejudice to an extreme, even by movie frontier standards."

295. Hunt, Dennis. [Review of TELL THEM WILLIE BOY IS HERE]. FILM QUARTERLY, 23 (Spring 1970): 60-61.

The film is a "reminder to white Americans that they are bigoted bastards who have been brutally mistreating the Indians"; the film is an exercise in white "self-flagellation."

296. Jeavens, Clyde. "THE RETURN OF A MAN CALLED HORSE." MONTHLY FILM BULLETIN, 43 (Nov. 1976): 234.

    Describes the film as pointless, condescending, and self-indulgent. The film has little authenticity in portraying tribal customs.

297. Johnson, William. "New Light on the Past: CHEYENNE AUTUMN." SENIOR SCHOLASTIC, 85 (Nov. 4, 1964): 30-31.

    Says Ford tries to show both sides of the winning of the West and in his films he pays tribute to the Cheyenne's heroic trek.

298. Kael, Pauline. "The Current Cinema: Americana." NEW YORKER, 45 (Dec. 27, 1969): 47-50.

    TELL THEM WILLIE BOY IS HERE is a film full of American self-hatred where the treatment of Indians is used symbolically to an excessive degree to represent American attitudes toward racial minorities.

299. Kael, Pauline. "The Current Cinema: Epic and Crumbcrusher." NEW YORKER, 46 (Dec. 26, 1970): 50-52.

    Finds Arthur Penn's LITTLE BIG MAN a film one wants to like but can't because the pieces just do not fit together, partly because it is "messagey" and partly because the slaughter is too reminiscent of Vietnam. Chief Dan George, "part patriarch, part Jewish mother," doesn't quite come off and neither do the hip comic bits with the Indians.

300. Kael, Pauline. "The Current Cinema: Star Mutations." NEW YORKER, 48 (Dec. 30, 1972): 50-51.

Describes JEREMIAH JOHNSON as something of a muddled movie with low-key performances by both the Indians and Redford. She finds Johnson's final gesture to the Crow chief a way for the moviemakers to unload white guilt for past actions toward the Indians.

301. Kael, Pauline. "The Current Cinema: Winging It." NEW YORKER, 47 (Nov. 27, 1971): 148-152.

Focuses on the female teacher in BILLY JACK, comparing her role to female film roles in general. Kael finds fault with the film but understands its appeal, particularly to young people.

302. Kaminsky, Stuart M. "ULZANA'S RAID." TAKE ONE, 3 (Jan.-Feb. 1972), 36-37.

Kaminsky understands Aldrich, the director, as trying to "fathom the Apache ever since 1954 when he made a film APACHE." We gain respect for Ulzana despite the growing atrocities. "The renegade Indian Ulzana emerges not simply as a figure of brutality and terror but as a consistent and honorable human being with a set of values so radically different from our own that we may never be able to understand them."

303. Kaufmann, Stanley. "Stanley Kaufmann on Films: BROKEN TREATY AT BATTLE MOUNTAIN." NEW REPUBLIC, 172 (Feb. 1, 1975): 20.

Calls the film "better than documentary . . . on the subject" and praises Joel Freedman's "objective sympathy."

304. Kaufmann, Stanley. "Stanley Kaufmann on Films: Bull Sitting." NEW REPUBLIC, 175 (July 24, 1976): 22.

Altman used Buffalo Bill's Wild West Show as a playground for his usual assumptive anti-Americanism and for the cinematic horseplay that he thinks endorses it.

305. Kaufmann, Stanley. "Stanley Kaufmann on Films: FLAP." NEW REPUBLIC, 164 (Jan. 23, 1971): 22.

Reviews FLAP as a corny ill-made picture full of tedious movie brawls and describes it as another pro-Indian, anti-white film.

306. Kaufmann, Stanley. "Stanley Kaufmann on Films: JEREMIAH JOHNSON." NEW REPUBLIC, 168 (Jan. 6 & 13, 1973): 24.

The treatment of Indians is evaluated as good in this film. Redford's Indian wife is described as really looking like an Indian girl, not a "starlet done up in Max Factor."

307. Kaufmann, Stanley. "Stanley Kaufmann on Films: LITTLE BIG MAN." NEW REPUBLIC, 123 (Dec. 26, 1970): 18.

Describes the reversal in LITTLE BIG MAN and gives as example the different audience expectations: "When Indians attack a stagecoach the murders are supposed to be funny; when cavalrymen attack an Indian village, the murders are tragic."

308. Kaufmann, Stanley. "Stanley Kaufmann on Films: No Ford in Our Future." NEW REPUBLIC, 152 (Jan. 23, 1965): 36-37.

   In this review of CHEYENNE AUTUMN, Kaufmann doesn't believe that the audience will buy Ford's attempt to gain sympathy for the Indians.

309. Keneas, Alex. "Indian Pudding." NEWSWEEK, 75 (May 25, 1970): 102, 104.

   "From its opening credit of the Smithsonian Institution archives to its extensive use of Sioux dialect, A MAN CALLED HORSE boasts an authentic vision of Indian life. Yet for all the teepee truism, its anthropological ancestor is Hollywood, where the Indian, proud but savage, became the RAISON D'ETRE for the cavalry charge."

310. Kindem, Gorham. "Towards a Semiotic of Color in Popular Narrative Films: Color Signification in John Ford's THE SEARCHERS." FILM READER, 2 (1977): 78-82.

   In this textual analysis of color in THE SEARCHERS, Kindem looks at color in relation to the narrative, time and space, and the original literary source for the film.

311. Klain, S. "BUFFALO BILL AND THE INDIANS." INDEPENDENT FILM JOURNAL, 78 (June 25, 1976): 13-14.

   Outlines the film's plot and evaluates Altman's success with the "unheroic" William F. Cody.

312. Knight, Arthur. [Review of FLAP]. SATURDAY REVIEW, 53 (Dec. 19, 1970): 38.

States that the picture "is an honest attempt to create sympathy for the Indians" and provides some detail of the lead character Flap and his actions.

313. Knight, Arthur. "A Man Called Camel." SATURDAY REVIEW, 53 (May 2, 1970): 52.

    Explains that Elliott Silverstein lost control over the final cut of A MAN CALLED HORSE and that it detracted from the authenticity of the whole. Nevertheless Knight finds the movie original and absorbing and the vivid action recalls the mute power of the silent screen which made the audience "look, absorb, and wonder at the exotic world so persuasively created out of shadow."

314. Knight, Arthur. "New Look at the Old West." SATURDAY REVIEW OF LITERATURE, 48 (Jan. 16, 1965): 36.

    John Ford is quoted as saying that he wanted the audience to meet the Indian face to face and get to know him and admire him in CHEYENNE AUTUMN.

315. Kroll, Jack. "Buffalo Bull." NEWSWEEK, 87 (June 28, 1976): 77.

    In this review of BUFFALO BILL AND THE INDIANS, Kroll comments, "only Altman could get such heartbreaking laughter out of racism as Buffalo Bill matches his bombast against the chief's mystic silences."

316. Kroll, Jack. "Out of the Sun." NEWSWEEK, 78 (August 30, 1971): 72.

    Despite the reviewers' general response that BILLY JACK is "corny and amateurish," Kroll praises its "naivete and innocence."

317. Lelchuk, Allen. "Mushville." ATLANTIC, 238 (Oct. 1976): 102-108.

In a negative review of BUFFALO BILL AND THE INDIANS, Lelchuk says, "the viewer is asked to accept that the white man means all things corrupt, material, evil, and the Indian all things spiritual, good, visionary."

318. Lockhart, Jane. [Review of BROKEN ARROW]. ROTARIAN, 77 (Nov. 1950): 36.

Recognizes that BROKEN ARROW is "something new" and represents a shift in attitude toward the American Indian.

319. McBride, Joseph, and Michael Wilmington. "Prisoner of the Desert." SIGHT AND SOUND, 40 (Autumn 1971): 210-214.

In this analysis of THE SEARCHERS and the role of Ethan Edwards, McBride and Wilmington describe the film as "a crystallization of the fears, obsessions and contradictions" which had been plaguing Ford since his return from World War II.

320. McBride, Joseph. "WINDWALKER." VARIETY, 301 (Dec. 10, 1980): 34.

Calls the film a "rare treat." All of the actors are American Indians except for Trevor Howard, and the dialogue in Cheyenne and Crow with English subtitles adds to the authenticity. The only flaw he sees is that Howard does not come off as an authentic Cheyenne in spite of his good acting.

321. Maslin, Janet. "Screen: Plains Warrior Reunites with His Son." NEW YORK TIMES, March 13, 1981, p. C12.

Finds WINDWALKER a film that breaks with the traditional Hollywood mold. She describes the story as enthralling instead of overdone and melodramatic.

322. Milne, Tom. "BUFFALO BILL AND THE INDIANS." SIGHT AND SOUND, 45 (Autumn 1976): 254.

Writes that Altman has deliberately decentralized any question of the reality of the Indian and the film becomes a confrontation of myth against myth.

323. Milne, Tom. "LITTLE BIG MAN." FOCUS ON FILM, 6 (Spring 1971): 3-7.

Sees the film as "a sociological treatise on the Cheyenne culture and customs, fascinating as well as thoroughly convincing for all that it might be pure fabrication."

324. Milne, Tom. "TELL THEM WILLIE BOY IS HERE." SIGHT AND SOUND, 39 (Spring 1970): 101-102.

Polonsky's theme is the fatalistic irony whereby Willie reverts to being an Indian when accused, in effect, of the crime of being an Indian. Willie becomes as alien and unfathomable as the painted, screaming scalp hunters who used to haunt the Hollywood Western. Milne describes the characters as so pared, the settings so subjugated to the image of bleak despair, that one begins to feel less than he should.

325. Morris, Gary. "THE SEARCHERS." BRIGHT LIGHTS, 2

(Fall 1977): 4-7.

THE SEARCHERS (1956) provides a study of the personality of Ethan Edwards (John Wayne) as a soldier returning from the Civil War only to find he has yet another battle to cope with, a battle within himself.

326. Murphey, A.D. "BUFFALO BILL AND THE INDIANS." VARIETY, 283 (June 30, 1976): 20.

In this negative review of the film, there is little mention made of the Indian roles.

327. Murphey, A.D. "THE WHITE BUFFALO." VARIETY, 288 (Sept. 21, 1977): 18.

Characterizes THE WHITE BUFFALO as a film with a poor script but big names. The dialogue can do little more than invite jeers.

328. Nachbar, Jack. "ULZANA'S RAID" in WESTERN MOVIES. Eds. William T. Pilkington and Don Graham. Albuquerque: University of New Mexico Press, 1979. Pp. 139-147.

Although neither as realistic, nor obviously mythic, nor technically innovative than a number of other Westerns of the early 1970s, ULZANA'S RAID is nevertheless important because it presented a dialectic rather than a "one-sided perspective on the Indian-white struggles on the closing of the frontier." The film is a summary of countless other Indian uprising films and provides a new direction for pictures of the future.

329. Nelson, Ralph. "Massacre at Sand Creek." FILMS AND FILMING, 16 (March 1970): 26-27.

REVIEWS

In this interview Nelson explains that he made SOLDIER BLUE because of the glossing over of the white American genocide of the Indians during the winning of the West.

330. Oberbeck, S.K. "U.S. Cavalry Go Home." NEWSWEEK, 76 (August 24, 1970): 65.

SOLDIER BLUE is seen as a gory film that doesn't strike deep enough at the heart of the prejudice it deals with, making the film too superficial.

331. Oulahan, Richard. "John Ford's Trojan Horse Opry." LIFE, 57 (Nov. 27, 1964): 19.

Praises CHEYENNE AUTUMN for showing the Indians as "heroes in a biblical exodus" and the whites as "paleface devils."

332. Patterson, F.T. "NANOOK OF THE NORTH." NEW REPUBLIC, 31 (August 9, 1922): 306-307.

Discusses the dramatic nature of the documentary about the Eskimo hunter Nanook.

333. Pechter, William S. "Altman, Chabrol, and Ray." COMMENTARY, 62 (Oct. 1976): 75-77.

BUFFALO BILL AND THE INDIANS is a moralizing tale about an American national hero who is a complete fraud and about the confusion caused by Sitting Bull's appearance. The show business lies prevail in the end, however, as the "venal white devils" trample the noble red man underfoot in the standard American demonology.

334. Pechter, William S. "Equal Time." COMMENTARY,

51 (April 1971): 80-81.

Describes LITTLE BIG MAN as "an Indian fighting Western with its conventional demonology reversed: bad white men riding against good Indians." Penn does not perceive that the problem is the demonology itself that brutalizes an audience and is the enemy of humane feeling.

335. Perkins, V.F. [Review of CHEYENNE AUTUMN]. MOVIE, No. 12 (Spring 1965): 36-37.

Asserts that this film demonstrates the studio's control over a filmmaker's material. The big money controls the contents of films by demanding consumer appeal. Warner Brothers tried to convert Ford's personal film into an epic and ruined the film's impact in doing so.

336. Rader, Dotson. [Review of SOLDIER BLUE]. NEW YORK TIMES, Sept. 20, 1970, pp. 11, 13.

Review of the film which Rader calls "powerful," "magnificent," and "the most brutal and liberating, the most honest American film ever made."

337. Ronan, Margaret. "Film." SENIOR SCHOLASTIC, 109 (Sept. 23, 1976): 12.

A short review that raises the question, "Is JEREMIAH JOHNSON really a symbol of the Indian tragedy?"

338. Ronan, Margaret. "Film: Lo, the True Indian!" SENIOR SCHOLASTIC, 96 (May 4, 1970): 24-25.

Believes that at last in A MAN CALLED HORSE the Indian breaks out of his dimension of defeat and

REVIEWS

takes his place in history.

339. Rosenbaum, Jonathan. "BUFFALO BILL AND THE INDIANS, OR SITTING BULL'S HISTORY LESSON." MONTHLY FILM BULLETIN, 43 (Sept. 1976): 188-189.

Praises the purposes of the film, but adds, "unfortunately, Altman appears to know a lot more about show business than about the American Indian."

340. Rosenbaum, Jonathan. "THE WHITE BUFFALO." MONTHLY FILM BULLETIN, 43 (Nov. 1976): 234.

Views the film as full of deadwood and plagued with incoherence. He says the film is not enjoyable or convincing.

341. Sarris, Andrew. "Bottom Line Buffalos Altman." VILLAGE VOICE, 21 (July 5, 1976): 107-109.

This article is more about Altman than BUFFALO BILL AND THE INDIANS, but gives some insight into the "behind the scenes" actions.

342. Scheuer, Philip K. "Indian's Culture Captured in Film." LOS ANGELES TIMES, May 21, 1950, pp. IV, 1-2.

In this review of BROKEN ARROW starring Jimmy Stewart and produced by Julien Blaustein, Blaustein explains he wanted "a documentary approach to a historical subject," so 375 Apaches from White River Reservation were hired for the movie. He believes the only "heavies" in this film are "ignorance, misunderstanding, and intolerance."

343. Schickel, Richard. "Bill Rendered." TIME, 108 (July 19, 1976): 66.

Review of BUFFALO BILL AND THE INDIANS which focuses mostly on Newman's portrayal of Buffalo Bill.

344. Schickel, Richard. "Critic's Roundup: TELL THEM WILLIE BOY IS HERE." LIFE, 67 (Nov. 28, 1969): 18.

 Describes Willie as James Dean in "Man-Tan" and the Indian girl as being of the "wooden, or cigar-store type."

345. Schickel, Richard. "Why Indians Can't Be Villains Anymore." NEW YORK TIMES, Feb. 9, 1975, pp. II, 1, 15.

 Uses ULZANA'S RAID to explore historical accuracy in portraying the Indian wars and concludes that those films showing brutality and savagism accurately portray the result of a cultural conflict that could never have been settled peacefully.

346. Shales, Tom. "THE VANISHING AMERICAN" in THE AMERICAN FILM HERITAGE. Ed. Kathleen Karr. Washington, DC: Acropolis Books, Ltd., 1972. Pp. 52-55.

 Describes the film as ahead of its time in its fairer and more empathetic view of the Indian than other films of the time. He calls the film "compassionate and impassioned cinema."

347. Sheperd, Duncan. "ULZANA'S RAID." CINEMA, 8 (Spring 1973): 44-45.

 Aldrich's film does not "tramp over previously surveyed territory." It does not "stretch beyond the Western genre's historical limits to gain a vantage point of enlightened hindsight," but it "revives the disreputable practice of stereotyping, with striking effects."

348. Simon, J. "Movies: Who is Buffaloing Whom?" NEW YORK, 9 (July 5, 1976): 70.

   Criticizes BUFFALO BILL AND THE INDIANS for "its consistently noble Indians and dependably ignoble whites."

349. Stabiner, Karen. "BUFFALO BILL AND THE INDIANS." FILM QUARTERLY, 30 (Fall 1976): 54-56.

   Sees the film as revealing the lies and legends of history and comments that what Altman examines is "the building of legends, heroes of American history who were always white, usually male, and undeniably omnipotent."

350. Stanbrook, Alan. "THE COVERED WAGON." FILMS AND FILMING, 6 (May 1960): 12-14, 35.

   The feature article on "Great Films of the Century" provides production details and plot outline for THE COVERED WAGON, a 1923 film of the epic crossing of America in 1849 by the biggest wagon train in history going west to Oregon.

351. Steinman, Clay. "The Method of THE SEARCHERS." UNIVERSITY FILM ASSOCIATION JOURNAL, 28 (1976): 19-24.

   In Ford's THE SEARCHERS (1956) photography reenforces the distance and isolation of Ethan Edwards.

352. Sufrin, Mark. [Review of WALK THE PROUD LAND].

SATURDAY REVIEW, 39 (August 25, 1956): 26.

Claims that this movie is one of the "Hollywood apology" types to make up for all of the unfair Indian films of the past. There is more discussion of the white man as negative than the Indian as positive.

353. Thompson, Howard. "FLAP, based on a Clair Huffaker Book, Opens." NEW YORK TIMES, Jan. 1, 1971, p.17.

Praises the arrival of a movie that deals with the contemporary American Indian. "The plight of the American Indian is no laughing matter. The laughter here makes it matter even more."

354. Turner, John W. "LITTLE BIG MAN: The Novel and the Film." LITERATURE/FILM QUARTERLY, 5 (Spring 1977): 154-163.

Argues that close examination of the novel illustrates some of the critical difficulties of the film, among them the use of the narrator, the identity problems of the central character, and the conflict between savagism and civilization.

355. Walbridge, Earl F. [Review of WALK THE PROUD LAND]. LIBRARY JOURNAL, 81 (Sept. 1, 1956): 1932.

Praises the film for adhering to historical fact and sees John Clum's treatment of the Indians on the San Carlos Indian reservation as tolerant and enlightened.

356. Walsh, Moria. "LITTLE BIG MAN." AMERICA, 124 (Jan. 30, 1971): 97.

Penn is able to include his awareness of the "injustice and atrocities inflicted on the Indians as the West was won" in an entertaining film that avoids "hindsight self-righteousness" and "wallowing in violence while pretending to decry it."

357. Walsh, Moria. "A MAN CALLED HORSE." AMERICA, 122 (May 16, 1970): 538, 540-541.

Argues that the film is a small foundation stone that by indirection "dramatizes the present plight of the Indians by portraying their past culture, its virtues as well as its unappetizing features, with some dignity and integrity."

358. Walsh, Moria. "More Loathsome Films." AMERICA, 123 (Sept. 19, 1970): 185-186.

Sees the film SOLDIER BLUE as a "fraud and an artistic mess and largely self-defeating." It is a "film that pretends to deny violence" while appealing "to the unspeculative forms of violence."

359. Walsh, Raoul. EACH MAN IN HIS TIME. New York: Farrar, Straus and Giroux, 1974. Pp. 324-327.

Walsh describes briefly the making of THEY DIED WITH THEIR BOOTS ON.

360. Westerbeck, Colin L., Jr. "All-American History." COMMONWEAL, 92 (Sept. 4, 1970): 441-442.

SOLDIER BLUE is a movie about a white woman liberated after two years of captivity by the Cheyennes. The film is characterized by gratuitous violence and confused motives.

361. Westerbeck, Colin L., Jr. "The Screen." COMMON-
WEAL, 103 (August 13, 1976): 528-529.

   In BUFFALO BILL AND THE INDIANS Altman has
   taken American history and folded it back against
   itself as if he wanted to make an enormous Rors-
   chach card out of it. In effect, his whole film
   is about the relationship between illusion and
   substance, fakery and the genuine article, and
   the difficulty of telling them apart.

362. Wood, Robin. "Arthur Penn in Canada." MOVIE,
18 (Winter 1970-71): 26-36.

   This interview with the director Arthur Penn
   contains some interesting information on the
   shooting of LITTLE BIG MAN, discusses how Penn
   kept the slangy language of Thomas Berger's novel
   for the Indians, and explains why he was able to
   create the moral tone of the film.

363. Yacowar, Maurice. "Private and Public Visions:
ZABRISKIE POINT and BILLY JACK." JOURNAL OF
POPULAR FILM, 1 (Summer 1972): 197-207.

   Believes BILLY JACK looks back to the American
   Indian for its values and detaches itself from
   the traditional treatment of Indians in films by
   becoming a rebuttal to the traditional Western.

364. Zimmerman, Paul D. "How the West Was Lost."
NEWSWEEK, 76 (Dec. 21, 1970): 98, 100.

   Describes Penn's LITTLE BIG MAN as a traditional
   Hollywood horse epic in spite of loving, human
   moments between Indian Dan George and white Dustin
   Hoffman.

Illustrations

1. *The Squaw Man* (1918)

2. *The Scarlet West* (1925)

3. Jim Thorpe with Carl Lemmele

4. *Buffalo Bill* (1944)

5. *They Died with Their Boots On* (1941)

6. *The Plainsman* (1936)

7. *The Unconquered* (1947)

8. *Northwest Passage* (1940)

9. *Seminole* (1953)

10. *Tonka* (1958)

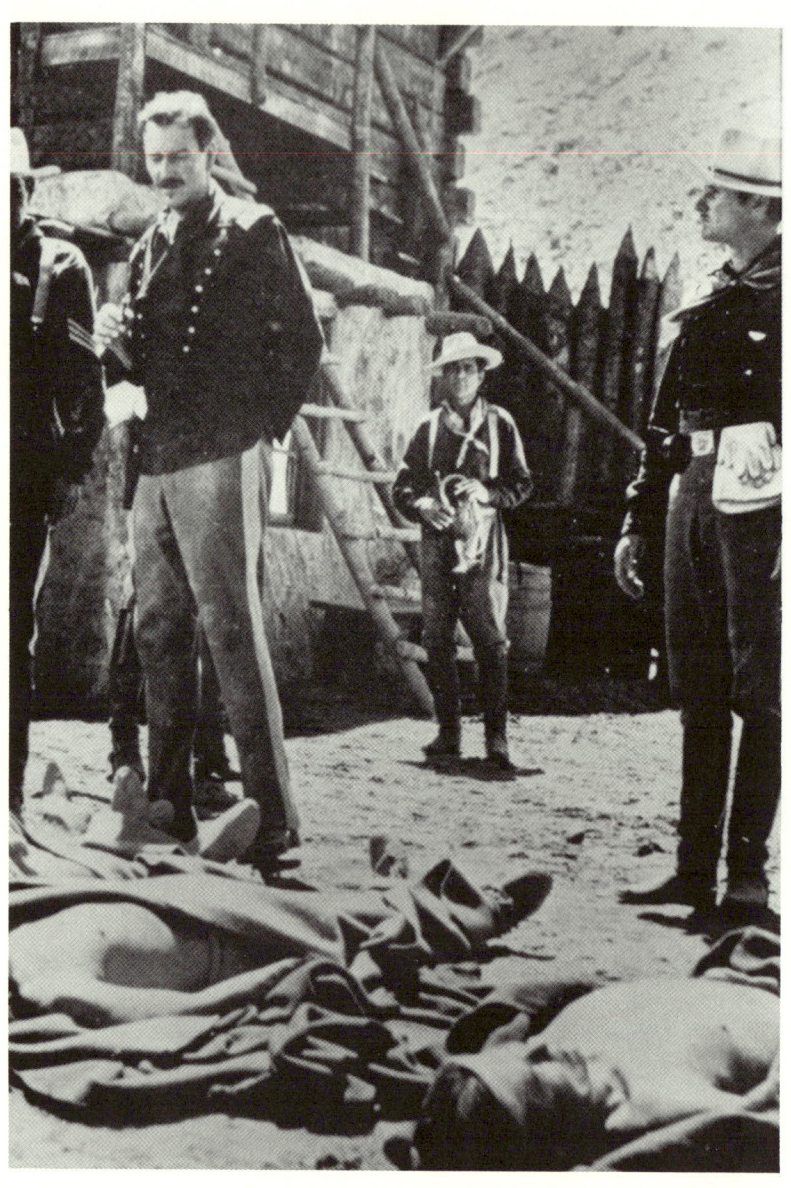

11. *Rio Grande* (1950)

12. *Cheyenne Autumn* (1964)

13. *Cheyenne Autumn* (1964)

14. *A Man Called Horse* (1970)

15. *The Way West* (1967)

16. *McKenna's Gold* (1969)

17. *Flap* (1970)

18. *Little Big Man* (1970)

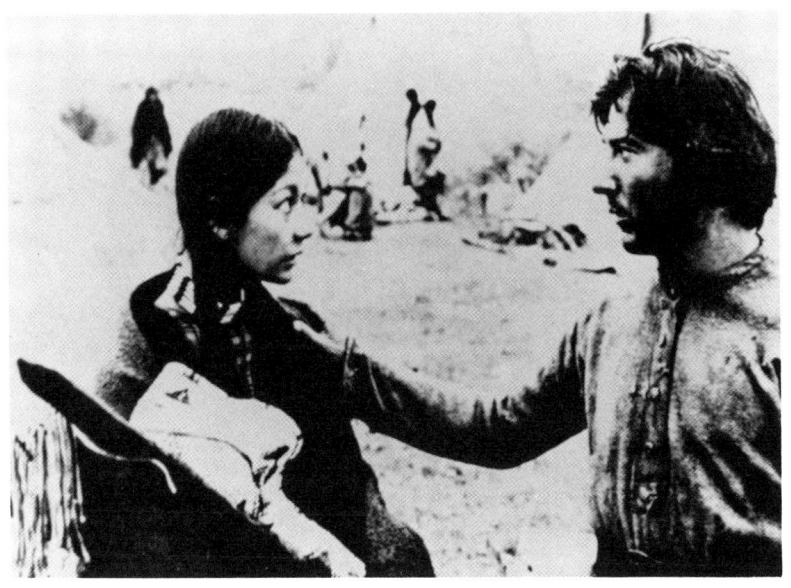

19. *Little Big Man* (1970)

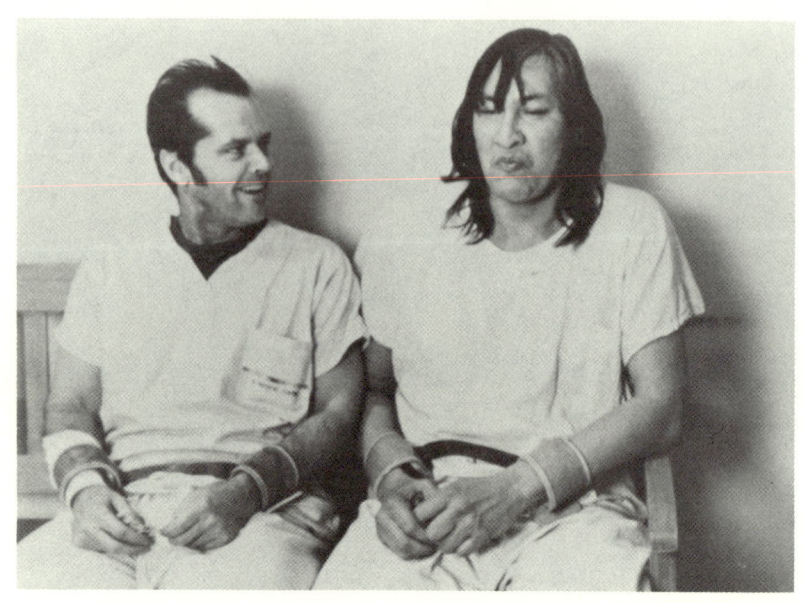

20. *One Flew Over the Cuckoo's Nest* (1975)

21. *Tell Them Willie Boy Is Here* (1969)

22. *Billy Jack* (1972)

23. *Jeremiah Johnson* (1972)

24. *White Buffalo* (1977)

25. *Broken Arrow* (1950)

26. *When the Legends Die* (1972)

27. *White Buffalo* (1977)

List of Sound Films Dealing
  with American Indians

List of Sound Films
Dealing with American Indians

1930-1939

365. THE BIG TRAIL (1930)
110m B-W
D: Raoul Walsh
S: John Wayne
Marguerite Churchill
El Brendel
Tully Marshall
Tyrone Power, Sr.
David Rollins
Ian Keith

366. THE RAINBOW TRAIL (1931)
58m B-W
D: Lynn Reynolds
S: Tom Mix
Anne Cornwall
George Bancroft
Lucien Littlefield
Mark Hamilton
Vivien Oakland

367. THE SQUAW MAN (1931)
105m B-W
D: Cecil B. DeMille
S: Paul Cavanagh
Lupe Valez
Eleanor Boardman
Cash Hawkins

Roland Young
Mitchell Lewis
Raymond Hatton

368. CALL HER SAVAGE (1932)
88m B-W
D: John Francis Dillon
S: Clara Bow
Monroe Owsley
Gilbert Roland
Thelma Todd
Estelle Taylor

369. THE GOLDEN WEST (1932)
74m B-W
D: David Howard
S: George O'Brien
Janet Chandler
Marion Burns
Arthur Pierson
Onslow Stevens

370. MASSACRE (1934)
70m B-W
D: Alan Crosland
S: Richard Barthelmess
Ann Dvorak
Dudley Digges
Claire Dodd
Henry O'Neill
Robert Barrat
Arthur Hohl
Sidney Toler
Clarence Muse

371. ANNIE OAKLEY (1935)
88m B-W
D: George Stevens
S: Barbara Stanwyck
Preston Foster
Melvyn Douglas
Pert Keltan
Andy Clyde

LIST OF FILMS

372. THE LAST OF THE MOHICANS (1936)
     91m B-W
     D: George B. Seitz
     S: Randolph Scott
        Binnie Barnes
        Heather Angel
        Hugh Buckler
        Henry Wilcoxon
        Bruce Cabot

373. THE PLAINSMAN (1936)
     115m B-W
     D: Cecil B. DeMille
     S: Gary Cooper
        Jean Arthur
        Charles Bickford
        James Ellison
        Porter Hall
        Victor Varconi
        Anthony Quinn

374. RAMONA (1936)
     90m C
     D: Henry King
     S: Loretta Young
        Don Ameche
        Kent Taylor
        Pauline Frederick
        Jane Darwell
        Katherine DeMille

375. ROSE MARIE (1936)
     110m B-W
     D: W.S. Van Dyke II
     S: Jeanette MacDonald
        Nelson Eddy
        Reginald Owen
        Allan Jones
        James Stewart
        Alan Mowbray
        Gilda Gray
     (Retitled: INDIAN LOVE CALL)

376. THE TEXAS RANGERS (1936)
    95m B-W
    D: King Vidor
    S: Fred MacMurray
       Jack Oakie
       Jean Parker
       Lloyd Nolan
       Edward Ellis

377. WAY OUT WEST (1937)
    65m B-W
    D: James W. Horne
    S: Stan Laurel
       Oliver Hardy
       Sharon Lynn
       James Finlay Lawrence
       Stanley Fields
       Vivien Oakland

378. WELLS FARGO (1937)
    94m B-W
    D: Frank Lloyd
    S: Joel McCrea
       Frances Dee
       Ralph Morgan
       Johnny Mack Brown
       Porter Hall
       Robert Cummings
       Harry Davenport

379. HAWK OF THE WILDERNESS (1938)
    100m B-W
    D: William Witney
    S: John English
       Bruce Bennett
       Mala
       Monte Blue
       Jill Martin
       Noble Johnson
    (Reedited movie serial: HAWK OF THE
                             WILDERNESS)

380. ALLEGHENY UPRISING (1939)

LIST OF FILMS   121

       81m B-W
       D: William Seiter
       S: John Wayne
          Claire Trevor
          George Sanders
          Brian Donlevy
          Robert Barrat
          Moroni Olsen
          Chill Wills

381.   DRUMS ALONG THE MOHAWK (1939)
       103m C
       D: John Ford
       S: Claudette Colbert
          Henry Fonda
          Edna May Oliver
          John Carradine
          Jessie Ralph
          Arthur Shields
          Robert Lowery
          Ward Bond

382.   GERONIMO (1939)
       89m B-W
       D: Paul H. Sloane
       S: Preston Foster
          Ellen Drew
          Andy Devine
          Gene Lockhart
          Ralph Morgan
          Marjorie Gateson
          Chief Thundercloud

383.   STAGECOACH (1939)
       99m B-W
       D: John Ford
       S: John Wayne
          Claire Trevor
          Thomas Mitchell
          Louise Platt
          Andy Devine
          George Bancroft
          John Carradine

Berton Churchill
Donald Meek

384. SUSANNAH OF THE MOUNTIES (1939)
 78m B-W
 D: William A. Seiter
 S: Shirley Temple
    Randolph Scott
    Margaret Lockwood
    J. Farrell MacDonald
    Moroni Olsen
    Victor Jory

385. UNION PACIFIC (1939)
 135m B-W
 D: Cecil B. DeMille
 S: Barbara Stanwyck
    Joel McCrea
    Robert Preston
    Brian Donlevy
    Anthony Quinn
    Lynne Overman
    Evelyn Keyes

1940-1949

386. GO WEST (1940)
 81m B-W
 D: Edward Buzzell
 S: Groucho Marx
    Chico Marx
    Harpo Marx
    John Carroll
    Dana Lewis
    Walter Woolf King
    Robert Barrat

387. KIT CARSON (1940)
 97m B-W
 D: George B. Seitz
 S: Jon Hall

LIST OF FILMS 123

>   Lynn Bari
>   Dana Andrews
>   Harold Huber
>   Ward Bond
>   Renie Riano
>   Clayton Moore

388. MY LITTLE CHICKADEE (1940)
     83m B-W
     D: Edward Cline
     S: Mae West
        W.C. Fields
        Joseph Calleia
        Dick Foran
        Ruth Donnelly
        Margaret Hamilton
        Donald Meek

389. NORTHWEST MOUNTED POLICE (1940)
     125m C
     D: Cecil B. DeMille
     S: Gary Cooper
        Madeleine Carroll
        Preston Foster
        Paulette Goddard
        Robert Preston
        George Bancroft

390. NORTHWEST PASSAGE (1940)
     125m C
     D: King Vidor
     S: Spencer Tracy
        Robert Young
        Walter Brennan
        Ruth Hussey
        Nat Pendleton
        Louis Hector
        Isabel Jewell
        Robert Barrat

391. BADLANDS OF DAKOTA (1941)
     74m B-W
     D: Alfred E. Green

S: Robert Stack
Ann Rutherford
Richard Dix
Frances Farmer
Broderick Crawford
Hugh Herbert

392. THEY DIED WITH THEIR BOOTS ON (1941)
138m B-W
D: Raoul Walsh
S: Errol Flynn
Olivia de Havilland
Arthur Kennedy
Charley Grapewin
Gene Lockhart
Anthony Quinn

393. WESTERN UNION (1941)
94m C
D: Fritz Lang
S: Robert Young
Randolph Scott
Dean Jagger
Virginia Gilmore
John Carradine
Slim Summerville
Chill Wills

394. RIDE 'EM COWBOY (1942)
86m B-W
D: Arthur Lubin
S: Bud Abbott
Lou Costello
Dick Foran
Anne Gwynne
Johnny Mack Brown
Ella Fitzgerald
Douglas Dumbrille

395. TEN GENTLEMEN FROM WEST POINT (1942)
102m B-W
D: Henry Hathaway
S: George Montgomery

LIST OF FILMS   125

        Maureen O'Hara
        John Sutton
        Laird Cregar
        Victor Francen
        Harry Davenport
        Ward Bond
        Tom Neal

396. VALLEY OF THE SUN (1942)
      84m B-W
      D: George Marshall
      S: Lucille Ball
         Cedric Hardwicke
         Dean Jagger
         James Craig
         Billy Gilbert
         Antonio Moreno

397. BUFFALO BILL (1944)
      90m C
      D: William Wellman
      S: Joel McCrea
         Maureen O'Hara
         Linda Darnell
         Thomas Mitchell
         Anthony Quinn
         Edgar Buchanan
         Chief Thundercloud
         Sidney Blackmer

398. BAD BASCOMB (1946)
      110m B-W
      D: S. Sylvan Simon
      S: Wallace Beery
         Margaret O'Brien
         Marjorie Main
         J. Carrol Naish
         Marshall Thompson

399. BADMAN'S TERRITORY (1946)
      97m B-W
      D: Tim Whelan
      S: Randolph Scott

Ann Richards
Gabby Hayes
Ray Collins
Chief Thundercloud

400. CANYON PASSAGE (1946)
99m C
D: Jacques Tourneur
S: Dana Andrews
Brian Donlevy
Susan Hayward
Ward Bond
Andy Devine
Lloyd Bridges

401. DUEL IN THE SUN (1946)
130m C
D: King Vidor
S: Jennifer Jones
Joseph Cotten
Gregory Peck
Lionel Barrymore
Lillian Gish
Herbert Marshall

402. MY DARLING CLEMENTINE (1946)
97m B-W
D: John Ford
S: Henry Fonda
Linda Darnell
Victor Mature
Walter Brennan
Tim Holt
Ward Bond
Alan Mowbray
John Ireland

403. BOWERY BUCKAROOS (1947)
66m B-W
D: William Beaudine
S: Leo Gorcey
Huntz Hall
Bobby Jordan

LIST OF FILMS   127

           Gabriel Dell
           Bill Benedict

404. KING OF THE WILD HORSES (1947)
      79m B-W
      D: George Archainbaud
      S: Preston Foster
         Gail Patrick
         Bill Sheffield
         Guinn Williams

405. LAST OF THE REDMEN (1947)
      77m C
      D: George Sherman
      S: Jon Hall
         Michael O'Shea
         Evelyn Ankers
         Julie Bishop
         Buster Crabbe

406. NORTHWEST OUTPOST (1947)
      91m B-W
      D: Allan Dwan
      S: Nelson Eddy
         Ilona Massey
         Hugo Haas
         Elsa Lanchester
         Lenore Ulric

407. UNCONQUERED (1947)
      146m C
      D: Cecil B. DeMille
      S: Gary Cooper
         Paulette Goddard
         Howard da Silva
         Boris Karloff
         Cecil Kellaway
         Ward Bond
         Katherine de Mille

408. BLOOD ON THE MOON (1948)
      88m B-W
      D: Robert Wise

       S: Robert Mitchum
          Barbara Bel Geddes
          Robert Preston
          Walter Brennan

409. THE DUDE GOES WEST (1948)
     87m B-W
     D: Kurt Neumann
     S: Eddie Albert
        Gale Storm
        James Gleason
        Binnie Barnes
        Gilbert Roland
        Barton MacLane

410. FORT APACHE (1948)
     127m B-W
     D: John Ford
     S: John Wayne
        Henry Fonda
        Shirley Temple
        Pedro Armendariz
        John Agar
        Anna Lee
        Ward Bond

411. FURY AT FURNACE CREEK (1948)
     88m B-W
     D: H. Bruce Humberstone
     S: Victor Mature
        Coleen Gray
        Glenn Langan
        Reginald Gardiner
        Albert Dekker

412. THE PALEFACE (1948)
     91m C
     D: Norman Z. McLeod
     S: Bob Hope
        Jane Russell
        Robert Armstrong
        Iris Adrian
        Robert Watson

LIST OF FILMS 129

Jack Searle

413. THE PLUNDERERS (1948)
 87m C
 D: Joseph Kane
 S: Rod Cameron
    Ilona Massey
    Adrian Booth
    Forrest Tucker

414. RACHEL AND THE STRANGER (1948)
 93m B-W
 D: Norman Foster
 S: Loretta Young
    William Holden
    Robert Mitchum
    Tom Tully
    Sara Haden

415. RED RIVER (1948)
 125m B-W
 D: Howard Hawks
 S: John Wayne
    Montgomery Cliff
    Joanne Dru
    Walter Brennan
    Coleen Gray
    John Ireland
    Harry Carey, Jr.
    Noah Beery, Jr.

416. SILVER RIVER (1948)
 110m B-W
 D: Raoul Walsh
 S: Errol Flynn
    Ann Sheridan
    Thomas Mitchell
    Bruce Bennett
    Tom D'Andrea

417. YELLOW SKY (1948)
 98m B-W
 D: William Wellman

S: Gregory Peck
   Anne Baxter
   Richard Widmark
   Robert Arthur
   John Russell
   Henry Morgan
   James Barton

418. AMBUSH (1949)
     89m B-W
     D: Sam Wood
     S: Robert Taylor
        John Hodiak
        Arlene Dahl
        Jean Hagen
        Chief Thundercloud

419. CANADIAN PACIFIC (1949)
     95m C
     D: Edwin L. Marin
     S: Randolph Scott
        Jane Wyatt
        J. Carrol Naish
        Victor Jory
        Nancy Olson

420. COLORADO TERRITORY (1949)
     94m B-W
     D: Raoul Walsh
     S: Joel McCrea
        Virginia Mayo
        Dorothy Malone
        Henry Hull
        John Archer
        Frank Puglia

421. LUST FOR GOLD (1949)
     90m B-W
     D: S. Sylvan Simon
     S: Ida Lupino
        Glenn Ford
        Jay Silverheels
        Eddy Waller

LIST OF FILMS 131

422. MASSACRE RIVER (1949)
    75m B-W
    D: John Rawlins
    S: Guy Madison
       Rory Calhoun
       Johnny Sands
       Carole Mathews
       Cathy Downs

423. MRS. MIKE (1949)
    99m B-W
    D: Louis King
    S: Dick Powell
       Evelyn Keyes
       J.M. Kerrigan
       Angela Clarke

424. SAND (1949)
    78m C
    D: Louis King
    S: Mark Stevens
       Rory Calhoun
       Coleen Gray
       Charley Grapewin
    (Retitled: WILL JAMES' SAND)

425. SHE WORE A YELLOW RIBBON (1949)
    103m C
    D: John Ford
    S: John Wayne
       Joanne Dru
       John Agar
       Ben Johnson
       Harry Carey, Jr.
       Victory McLaglen
       Mildred Natwick

426. TULSA (1949)
    90m C
    D: Stuart Heisler
    S: Susan Hayward
       Robert Preston
       Pedro Armendariz

Lloyd Gough
Chill Wills
Ed Begley

1950-1959

427. ANNIE GET YOUR GUN (1950)
    107m C
    D: George Sidney
    S: Betty Hutton
       Howard Keel
       Louis Calhern
       Edward Arnold
       Keenan Wynn

428. BROKEN ARROW (1950)
    93m C
    D: Delmer Daves
    S: James Stewart
       Jeff Chandler
       Debra Paget
       Will Geer
       Jay Silverheels

429. THE CARIBOO TRAIL (1950)
    81m C
    D: Edwin L. Marin
    S: Randolph Scott
       George "Gabby" Hayes
       Bill Williams
       Karin Booth
       Victor Jory

430. COMANCHE TERRITORY (1950)
    76m C
    D: George Sherman
    S: Maureen O'Hara
       Macdonald Carey
       Will Geer
       James Best
       Edmund Cobb

LIST OF FILMS 133

431. DAVY CROCKETT--INDIAN SCOUT (1950)
 71m B-W
 D: Lew Landers
 S: George Montgomery
    Ellen Drew
    Philip Reed
    Chief Thundercloud

432. DEVIL'S DOORWAY (1950)
 84m B-W
 D: Anthony Mann
 S: Robert Taylor
    Louis Calhern
    Paula Raymond
    Marshall Thompson

433. THE IROQUOIS TRAIL (1950)
 85m B-W
 D: Phil Karlson
 S: George Montgomery
    Brenda Marshall
    Dan O'Herlihy
    Glenn Langen

434. THE OUTRIDERS (1950)
 93m C
 D: Roy Rowland
 S: Joel McCrea
    Arlene Dahl
    Barry Sullivan
    Claude Jarman, Jr.
    Ramon Novarro

435. RIO GRANDE (1950)
 105m B-W
 D: John Ford
 S: John Wayne
    Maureen O'Hara
    Ben Johnson
    Harry Carey, Jr.
    Victor McLaglen
    Claude Jarman, Jr.

436. ROCKY MOUNTAIN (1950)
    83m B-W
    D: William Keighley
    S: Errol Flynn
       Patrice Wymore
       Scott Forbes
       Slim Pickens
       Sheb Wooley
       Yakima Canutt

437. A TICKET TO TOMAHAWK (1950)
    90m C
    D: Richard Sale
    S: Dan Daily
       Anne Baxter
       Rory Calhoun
       Walter Brennan
       Marilyn Monroe
       Chief Yowlachie

438. THE TRAVELING SALESWOMAN (1950)
    75m B-W
    D: Charles F. Riesner
    S: Joan Davis
       Andy Devine
       Adele Jergens
       Chief Thundercloud

439. TWO FLAGS WEST (1950)
    92m B-W
    D: Robert Wise
    S: Joseph Cotton
       Linda Darnell
       Jeff Chandler
       Cornel Wilde
       Dale Robertson

440. WAGON MASTER (1950)
    86m B-W
    D: John Ford
    S: Ben Johnson
       Joanne Dru
       Ward Bond

LIST OF FILMS 135

        Alan Mowbray
        Jane Darwell
        James Arness

441. WINCHESTER '73 (1950)
     92m B-W
     D: Anthony Mann
     S: James Stewart
        Shelley Winters
        Dan Duryea
        Rock Hudson
        Tony Curtis

442. YOUNG DANIEL BOONE (1950)
     71m C
     D: Reginald LeBorg
     S: David Bruce
        Kristine Miller
        Mary Treen
        Don Beddoe

443. ACROSS THE WIDE MISSOURI (1951)
     78m C
     D: William Wellman
     S: Clark Gable
        Ricardo Montalban
        John Hodiak
        Adolphe Menjou

444. APACHE DRUMS (1951)
     75m C
     D: Hugo Fregonese
     S: Stephen McNally
        Coleen Gray
        Willard Parker
        Arthur Shields

445. CAVALRY SCOUT (1951)
     78m C
     D: Lesley Selander
     S: Rod Cameron
        Audrey Long
        Jim Davis

James Millican

446. DISTANT DRUMS (1951)
    101m C
    D: Raoul Walsh
    S: Gary Cooper
       Mari Aldon
       Richard Webb
       Ray Teal

447. FLAMING FEATHER (1951)
    77m C
    D: Ray Enright
    S: Sterling Hayden
       Forrest Tucker
       Barbara Rush
       Arleen Whelan

448. FORT DEFIANCE (1951)
    81m C
    D: John Rawlins
    S: Dane Clark
       Ben Johnson
       Peter Graves
       Tracey Roberts

449. JIM THORPE--ALL AMERICAN (1951)
    107m B-W
    D: Michael Curtiz
    S: Burt Lancaster
       Charles Bickford
       Steve Cochran
       Phyllis Thaxter

450. THE LAST OUTPOST (1951)
    88m C
    D: Lewis R. Foster
    S: Ronald Reagan
       Rhonda Fleming
       Bruce Bennett
       Bill Williams

451. LITTLE BIG HORN (1951)

LIST OF FILMS 137

    86m B-W
    D: Charles Marquis Warren
    S: Lloyd Bridges
       John Ireland
       Marie Windsor
       Reed Hadley

452. NEW MEXICO (1951)
    76m C
    D: Irving Reis
    S: Lew Ayres
       Marilyn Maxwell
       Robert Hutton
       Andy Devine
       Raymond Burr

453. OH! SUSANNA (1951)
    90m C
    D: Joseph Kane
    S: Rod Cameron
       Forrest Tucker
       Adrian Booth
       Chill Wills

454. ONLY THE VALIANT (1951)
    105m B-W
    D: Gordon Douglas
    S: Gregory Peck
       Barbara Payton
       Ward Bond
       Gig Young
       Lon Chaney
       Neville Brand
       Jeff Corey

455. RED MOUNTAIN (1951)
    84m C
    D: William Dieterle
    S: Alan Ladd
       Lizabeth Scott
       John Ireland
       Arthur Kennedy

456. SLAUGHTER TRAIL (1951)
    78m C
    D: Irving Allen
    S: Brian Donlevy
       Gig Young
       Virginia Grey
       Andy Devine

457. STREETS OF LAREDO (1951)
    68m C
    D: Phil Karlson
    S: George Montgomery
       Gale Storm
       Jerome Courtland
       Noah Beery, Jr.

458. TOMAHAWK (1951)
    82m C
    D: George Sherman
    S: Yvonne DeCarlo
       Van Heflin
       Preston Foster
       Jack Oakie
       Alex Nicol

459. WARPATH (1951)
    95m C
    D: Bryon Haskin
    S: Edmond O'Brien
       Dean Jagger
       Forrest Tucker
       Polly Bergen

460. WESTWARD THE WOMEN (1951)
    118m B-W
    D: William Wellman
    S: Robert Taylor
       Denise Darcel
       Beverly Dennis
       John McIntire
       Hope Emerson
       Lenore Lonergan
       Julie Bishop

LIST OF FILMS 139

>   Marilyn Erskine

461. WHEN THE REDSKINS RODE (1951)
     78m C
     D: Lew Landers
     S: Jon Hall
        Mary Castle
        James Seay
        John Ridgley

462. APACHE WAR SMOKE (1952)
     67m B-W
     D: Howard F. Kress
     S: Gilbert Roland
        Robert Horton
        Glenda Farrell
        Gene Lockhart
        Bobby Blake

463. THE BATTLE AT APACHE PASS (1952)
     85m C
     D: George Sherman
     S: Jeff Chandler
        John Lund
        Beverly Tyler
        Richard Egan
        Hugh O'Brian
        Jay Silverheels

464. BEND OF THE RIVER (1952)
     91m C
     D: Anthony Mann
     S: James Stewart
        Julia Adams
        Rock Hudson
        Arthur Kennedy
        Stepin Fetchit

465. THE BIG SKY (1952)
     122m B-W
     D: Howard Hawks
     S: Kirk Douglas
        Dewey Martin

Arthur Hunnicutt
Jim Davis

466. BRAVE WARRIOR (1952)
 73m C
 D: Spencer G. Bennett
 S: Jon Hall
    Jay Silverheels
    Michael Ansara
    Christine Larson

467. BUGLES IN THE AFTERNOON (1952)
 85m C
 D: Roy Rowland
 S: Ray Milland
    Forrest Tucker
    George Reeves
    Helena Carter
    Gertrude Michael

468. FORT OSAGE (1952)
 72m C
 D: Lesley Selander
 S: Rod Cameron
    Jane Nigh
    Douglas Kennedy

469. THE HALF-BREED (1952)
 81m C
 D: Lewis D. Collins
 S: Robert Young
    Janis Carter
    Jack Buetel
    Barton MacLane
    Porter Hall

470. INDIAN UPRISING (1952)
 75m C
 D: Ray Nazarro
 S: George Montgomery
    Audrey Long
    Carol Benton Reid
    Robert Shayne

LIST OF FILMS

471. LAST OF THE COMANCHES (1952)
     85m C
     D: Andre de Toth
     S: Broderick Crawford
        Barbara Hale
        Lloyd Bridges
        Martin Milner
        John War Eagle

472. LONE STAR (1952)
     94m B-W
     D: Vincent Sherman
     S: Clark Gable
        Ava Gardner
        Lionel Barrymore
        Beulah Bondi
        Broderick Crawford
        Ed Begley

473. THE PATHFINDER (1952)
     78m C
     D: Sidney Salkow
     S: George Montgomery
        Helena Carter
        Jay Silverheels
        Elena Verdugo
        Chief Yowlachie

474. PONY SOLDIER (1952)
     82m C
     D: Joseph M. Newman
     S: Tyrone Power
        Cameron Mitchell
        Robert Horton
        Thomas Gomez
        Penny Edwards

475. THE SAVAGE (1952)
     95m C
     D: George Marshall
     S: Charlton Heston
        Susan Morrow
        Peter Hanson

Joan Taylor
Ted de Corsia

476. THE SON OF PALEFACE (1952)
95m C
D: Frank Tashlin
S: Bob Hope
Jane Russell
Roy Rogers
Bill Williams
Harry von Zell
Iron Eyes Cody

477. THE WILD NORTH (1952)
97m C
D: Andrew Marton
S: Stewart Granger
Cyd Charisse
Wendell Corey
J.M. Kerrigan
Ray Teal

478. AMBUSH AT TOMAHAWK GAP (1953)
73m C
D: Fred F. Sears
S: John Hodiak
John Derek
David Brian
Percy Helton
Maria Elena Marques

479. ARROWHEAD (1953)
105m B-W
D: Charles Marquis Warren
S: Charlton Heston
Jack Palance
Katy Jurado
Brian Keith
Milburn Stone

480. CAPTAIN JOHN SMITH AND POCAHONTAS (1953)
75m C
D: Lew Landers

LIST OF FILMS   143

           S: Anthony Dexter
               Jody Lawrence
               Alan Hale, Jr.
               Douglas Dumbrille

481.   THE CHARGE AT FEATHER RIVER (1953)
       96m C (3-D)
       D: Gordon Douglas
       S: Guy Madison
           Vera Miles
           Frank Lovejoy
           Helen Westcott
           Ron Hagerthy

482.   COLUMN SOUTH (1953)
       85m C
       D: Frederick de Cordova
       S: Audie Murphy
           Joan Evans
           Robert Sterling
           Ray Collins

483.   CONQUEST OF COCHISE (1953)
       70m C
       D: William Castle
       S: John Hodiak
           Robert Stack
           Joy Page
           John Crawford

484.   ESCAPE FROM FORT BRAVO (1953)
       98m C
       D: John Sturges
       S: William Holden
           Eleanor Parker
           John Forsythe
           Polly Bergen
           William Demarest

485.   FORT TI (1953)
       73m C (3-D)
       D: William Castle
       S: George Montgomery

Joan Vohs
Irving Bacon
James Seay

486. FORT VENGEANCE (1953)
75m B-W
D: Lesley Selander
S: James Craig
Rita Moreno
Keith Larsen
Reginald Denny
Emory Parnell

487. THE GREAT SIOUX UPRISING (1953)
80m C
D: Lloyd Bacon
S: Jeff Chandler
Faith Domerque
Lyle Bettger
Glen Strange

488. HONDO (1953)
84m C (3-D)
D: John Farrow
S: John Wayne
Geraldine Page
Ward Bond
James Arness
Lee Aaker

489. JACK MCCALL, DESPERADO (1953)
76m C
D: Sidney Salkow
S: George Montgomery
Angela Stevens
Jay Silverheels
Douglas Kennedy

490. THE NEBRASKAN (1953)
68m C
D: Fred F. Sears
S: Phil Carey
Roberta Haynes

LIST OF FILMS 145

        Wallace Ford
        Richard Webb
        Lee Van Cleef
        Jay Silverheels

491. PONY EXPRESS (1953)
    101m C
    D: Jerry Hopper
    S: Charlton Heston
       Rhonda Fleming
       Jan Sterling
       Forrest Tucker

492. SEMINOLE (1953)
    87m C
    D: Budd Boetticher
    S: Rock Hudson
       Barbara Hale
       Anthony Quinn
       Richard Carlson
       Hugh O'Brien

493. STAND AT APACHE RIVER (1953)
    77m C
    D: Lee Sholem
    S: Stephen McNally
       Julia Adams
       Hugh Marlowe
       Jack Kelly
       Hugh O'Brian

494. TUMBLEWEED (1953)
    79m C
    D: Nathan Juran
    S: Audie Murphy
       Lori Nelson
       Chill Wills
       Lee Van Cleef

495. WAR ARROW (1953)
    78m C
    D: George Sherman
    S: Maureen O'Hara

        Jeff Chandler
        Suzan Ball
        Charles Drake
        Jay Silverheels

496. WAR PAINT (1953)
    89m C
    D: Lesley Selander
    S: Robert Stack
       Joan Taylor
       Charles McGraw
       Peter Graves

497. APACHE (1954)
    91m C
    D: Robert Aldrich
    S: Burt Lancaster
       Jean Peters
       John McIntire
       Charles (Bronson) Buchinsky

498. ARROW IN THE DUST (1954)
    80m B-W
    D: Lesley Selander
    S: Sterling Hayden
       Coleen Gray
       Keith Larsen
       Tom Tully

499. THE BATTLE OF ROGUE RIVER (1954)
    71m C
    D: William Castle
    S: George Montgomery
       Richard Denning
       Martha Hyer
       John Crawford

500. THE BLACK DAKOTAS (1954)
    65m C
    D: Ray Nazarro
    S: Gary Merrill
       Wanda Hendrix
       John Bromfield

LIST OF FILMS 147

        Noah Beery, Jr.

501. BROKEN LANCE (1954)
96m C
D: Edward Dmytryk
S: Spencer Tracy
Robert Wagner
Jean Peters
Richard Widmark

502. CATTLE QUEEN OF MONTANA (1954)
88m C
D: Allan Dwan
S: Barbara Stanwyck
Ronald Reagan
Gene Evans
Lance Fuller

503. THE COMMAND (1954)
88m C
D: David Butler
S: Guy Madison
Joan Weldon
James Whitmore
Carl Benton Reid

504. DANGEROUS MISSION (1954)
75m C
D: Louis King
S: Victor Mature
Piper Laurie
Vincent Price
William Bendix
Betta St. John

505. DRUM BEAT (1954)
111m C
D: Delmer Daves
S: Alan Ladd
Audrey Dalton
Marisa Pavan
Robert Keith

506. DRUMS ACROSS THE RIVER (1954)
 78m C
 D: Nathan Juran
 S: Audie Murphy
    Lisa Gaye
    Walter Brennan
    Lyle Bettger

507. FOUR GUNS TO THE BORDER (1954)
 82m C
 D: Richard Carlson
 S: Rory Calhoun
    Colleen Miller
    George Nader
    Walter Brennan
    Nina Foch

508. GARDEN OF EVIL (1954)
 100m C
 D: Henry Hathaway
 S: Gary Cooper
    Susan Hayward
    Richard Widmark
    Hugh Marlowe
    Cameron Mitchell
    Rita Moreno

509. MASTERSON OF KANSAS (1954)
 73m C
 D: William Castle
 S: George Montgomery
    Nancy Gates
    James Griffith
    Jean Willes
    Benny Rubin

510. OVERLAND PACIFIC (1954)
 73m C
 D: Fred F. Sears
 S: Jock Mahoney
    Peggy Castle
    Adele Jergens
    William Bishop

LIST OF FILMS   149

511. RIVER OF NO RETURN (1954)
     91m C
     D: Otto Preminger
     S: Robert Mitchum
        Marilyn Monroe
        Rory Calhoun
        Rommy Rettig
        Murvyn Vye

512. ROSE MARIE (1954)
     115m C
     D: Mervyn LeRoy
     S: Ann Blyth
        Howard Keel
        Fernando Lamas
        Bert Lahr
        Marjorie Main
        Joan Taylor
        Ray Collins

513. SASKATCHEWAN (1954)
     87m C
     D: Raoul Walsh
     S: Alan Ladd
        Shelley Winters
        J. Carrol Naish
        Hugh O'Brian
        Robert Douglas

514. SIEGE AT RED RIVER (1954)
     81m C
     D: Rudolph Mate
     S: Van Johnson
        Joanne Dru
        Richard Boone
        Milburn Stone
        Jeff Morrow

515. SITTING BULL (1954)
     105m C
     D: Sidney Salkow
     S: Dale Robertson
        Mary Murphy

J. Carrol Naish
Iron Eyes Cody
John Litel

516. SOUTHWEST PASSAGE (1954)
 82m C
 D: Ray Nazarro
 S: Rod Cameron
    John Ireland
    John Dehner
    Guinn Williams
    Mark Hanna

517. TAZA, SON OF COCHISE (1954)
 79m C
 D: Douglas Sirk
 S: Rock Hudson
    Barbara Rush
    Gregg Palmer
    Bart Roberts
    Morris Ankrum

518. THEY RODE WEST (1954)
 84m C
 D: Phil Karlson
 S: Robert Francis
    Donna Reed
    May Wynn
    Phil Carey
    Onslow Stevens

519. THREE YOUNG TEXANS (1954)
 78m C
 D: Henry Levin
 S: Mitzi Gaynor
    Keefe Brasselle
    Jeffrey Hunter
    Harvey Stephens
    Dan Riss

520. THUNDER PASS (1954)
 76m B-W
 D: Frank McDonald

LIST OF FILMS   151

         S: Dane Clark
             Andy Devine
             Dorothy Patrick
             Raymond Burr

521. YELLOW TOMAHAWK (1954)
      82m C
      D: Lesley Selander
      S: Rory Calhoun
          Peggy Castle
          Noah Beery
          Warner Anderson

522. APACHE AMBUSH (1955)
      68m B-W
      D: Fred F. Sears
      S: Bill Williams
          Richard Jaeckel
          Movita
          Tex Ritter

523. BATTLE CRY (1955)
      149m C
      D: Raoul Walsh
      S: Van Heflin
          Tab Hunter
          Dorothy Malone
          Anne Francis
          Raymond Massey
          Mona Freeman
          Aldo Ray

524. CHIEF CRAZY HORSE (1955)
      86m C
      D: George Sherman
      S: Victor Mature
          Suzan Ball
          John Lund
          Ray Danton
          Keith Larsen

525. DAVY CROCKETT, KING OF THE WILD FRONTIER
      (1955)

93m C
D: Norman Foster
S: Fess Parker
   Buddy Ebsen
   Basil Ruysdael
   Hans Conried

526. THE FAR HORIZONS (1955)
     108m C
     D: Rudolph Mate
     S: Fred MacMurray
        Charlton Heston
        Donna Reed
        Barbara Hale
        William Demarest

527. FORT YUMA (1955)
     78m C
     D: Lesley Selander
     S: Peter Graves
        Joan Taylor
        Addison Richards
        Joan Vohs

528. FOXFIRE (1955)
     92m C
     D: Joseph Pevney
     S: Jane Russell
        Jeff Chandler
        Dan Duryea
        Mara Corday
        Barton MacLane

529. THE GUN THAT WON THE WEST (1955)
     71m C
     D: William Castle
     S: Dennis Morgan
        Paula Raymond
        Richard Denning
        Robert Bice

530. THE INDIAN FIGHTER (1955)
     88m C

LIST OF FILMS 153

    D: Andre de Toth
    S: Kirk Douglas
       Walter Matthau
       Elsa Martinelli
       Walter Abel
       Lon Chaney

531. KISS OF FIRE (1955)
    87m C
    D: Joseph M. Newman
    S: Barbara Rush
       Jack Palance
       Rex Reason
       Martha Hyer

532. THE LAST FRONTIER (1955)
    98m C
    D: Anthony Mann
    S: Victor Mature
       Guy Madison
       Robert Preston
       James Whitmore
       Anne Bancroft

533. THE MAN FROM LARAMIE (1955)
    104m C
    D: Anthony Mann
    S: James Stewart
       Arthur Kennedy
       Donald Crisp
       Cathy O'Donnell
       Alex Nicol
       Aline MacMahon
       Wallace Ford

534. MANY RIVERS TO CROSS (1955)
    92m C
    D: Roy Rowland
    S: Robert Taylor
       Eleanor Parker
       Victor McLaglen
       James Arness
       Josephine Hutchinson

535. SANTA FE PASSAGE (1955)
 70m C
 D: William Witney
 S: John Payne
    Faith Domerque
    Rod Cameron
    Slim Pickens

536. SEMINOLE UPRISING (1955)
 74m C
 D: Earl Bellamy
 S: George Montgomery
    Karin Booth
    John Pickard
    Ed Hinton

537. SEVEN CITIES OF GOLD (1955)
 103m C
 D: Robert D. Webb
 S: Richard Egan
    Anthony Quinn
    Jeffrey Hunter
    Rita Moreno
    Michael Rennie

538. SHOTGUN (1955)
 81m C
 D: Lesley Selander
 S: Sterling Hayden
    Zachary Scott
    Yvonne De Carlo
    Guy Prescott
    Angela Greene

539. STRANGE LADY IN TOWN (1955)
 112m C
 D: Mervyn LeRoy
 S: Greer Garson
    Dana Andrews
    Cameron Mitchell
    Lois Smith
    Walter Hampden

LIST OF FILMS 155

540. THE TALL MEN (1955)
    122m C
    D: Raoul Walsh
    S: Clark Gable
       Jane Russell
       Robert Tryan
       Cameron Mitchell
       Mae Marsh

541. THE TWINKLE IN GOD'S EYES (1955)
    73m B-W
    D: George Blair
    S: Mickey Rooney
       Coleen Gray
       Hugh O'Brian
       Joey Forman
       Michael Connors

542. THE VANISHING AMERICAN (1955)
    90m B-W
    D: Joseph Kane
    S: Scott Brady
       Audrey Totter
       Forrest Tucker
       Gene Lockhart
       Jim Davis
       Jay Silverheels

543. WHITE FEATHER (1955)
    102m C
    D: Robert D. Webb
    S: Robert Wagner
       Jeffrey Hunter
       Debra Paget
       John Lund
       Eduard Franz
       Hugh O'Brian

544. AROUND THE WORLD IN 80 DAYS (1956)
    167m C
    D: Michael Anderson
    S: David Niven
       Cantinflas

Shirley MacLaine
Robert Newton
Marlene Dietrich

545. BACKLASH (1956)
84m C
D: John Sturges
S: Richard Widmark
Donna Reed
William Campbell
John McIntire
Barton MacLane

546. CANYON RIVER (1956)
80m C
D Harmon Jones
S: George Montgomery
Marcia Henderson
Peter Graves
Richard Eyer

547. COMANCHE (1956)
87m C
D: George Sherman
S: Dana Andrews
Kent Smith
Linda Cristal
Nestor Paiva
Henry Brandon

548. DAKOTA INCIDENT (1956)
88m C
D: Lewis R. Foster
S: Linda Darnell
Dale Robertson
John Lund
Ward Bond

549. DANIEL BOONE, TRAIL BLAZER (1956)
76m C
D: Albert C. Gannaway
S: Ismael Rodriquez
Bruce Bennett

LIST OF FILMS 157

        Lon Chaney
        Faron Young
        Ken Dibbs

550. GREAT DAY IN THE MORNING (1956)
     92m C
     D: Jacques Tourneur
     S: Virginia Mayo
        Robert Stack
        Ruth Roman
        Alex Nicol
        Raymond Burr

551. THE LAST HUNT (1956)
     108m C
     D: Richard Brooks
     S: Robert Taylor
        Stewart Granger
        Lloyd Noland
        Debra Paget
        Russ Tamblyn
        Constance Ford

552. THE LAST WAGON (1956)
     99m C
     D: Delmer Daves
     S: Richard Widmark
        Felicia Farr
        Susan Kohner
        Tommy Rettig
        Stephanie Griffin
        Ray Stricklyn
        Nick Adams

553. THE LONE RANGER (1956)
     86m C
     D: Stuart Heisler
     S: Clayton Moore
        Jay Silverheels
        Lyle Bettger
        Bonita Granville
        Perry Lopez
        Robert Wilke

554. MASSACRE (1956)
     75m C
     D: Louis King
     S: Dane Clark
        James Craig
        Marta Roth
        Jaime Fernandez
        Ferrusquilla
        Miguel Torruco
        Jose Munoz
        Enrique Zambrano

555. MOHAWK (1956)
     79m C
     D: Kurt Neumann
     S: Scott Brady
        Rita Gam
        Neville Brand
        Lori Nelson
        Allison Hayes

556. PILLARS OF THE SKY (1956)
     95m C
     D: George Marshall
     S: Jeff Chandler
        Dorothy Malone
        Ward Bond
        Keith Andes
        Lee Marvin
        Sydney Chaplin

557. THE PROUD AND THE PROFANE (1956)
     111m B-W
     D: George Seaton
     S: William Holden
        Deborah Kerr
        Thelma Ritter
        Dewey Martin

558. REPRISAL (1956)
     74m C
     D: George Sherman
     S: Guy Madison

LIST OF FILMS 159

        Felicia Farr
        Kathryn Grant
        Michael Pate
        Edward Platt

559. THE SEARCHERS (1956)
    119m C
    D: John Ford
    S: John Wayne
       Jeffrey Hunter
       Vera Miles
       Ward Bond
       Natalie Wood
       John Qualen
       Harry Carey, Jr.
       Olive Carey
       Antonio Moreno
       Dorothy Jordan

560. THE SECRET OF TREASURE MOUNTAIN (1956)
    68m B-W
    D: Seymour Friedman
    S: Valerie French
       Raymond Burr
       William Prince
       Lance Fuller
       Susan Cummings

561. SEVENTH CAVALRY (1956)
    75m C
    D: Joseph H. Lewis
    S: Randolph Scott
       Barbara Hale
       Jay C. Flippen
       Jeanette Nolan
       Frank Faylen

562. WALK THE PROUD LAND (1956)
    88m C
    D: Jesse Hibbs
    S: Audie Murphy
       Anne Bancroft
       Pat Crowley

Charles Drake

563. WESTWARD HO THE WAGONS! (1956)
     90m C
     D: William Beaudine
     S: Fess Parker
        Kathleen Crowley
        Jeff York
        David Stollery
        Sebastian Cabot
        George Reeves

564. THE WHITE SQUAW (1956)
     75m B-W
     D: Ray Nazarro
     S: David Brian
        May Wynn
        William Bishop
        Nancy Hale

565. APACHE WARRIOR (1957)
     74m B-W
     D: Elmo Williams
     S: Keith Larsen
        Jim Davis
        Michael Carr
        Eddie Little

566. DRAGON WELLS MASSACRE (1957)
     88m C
     D: Harold Schuster
     S: Barry Sullivan
        Dennis O'Keefe
        Mona Freeman
        Katy Jurado
        Sebastian Cabot

567. HALLIDAY BRAND (1957)
     77m B-W
     D: Joseph H. Lewis
     S: Joseph Cotten
        Viveca Lindfors
        Betsy Blair

LIST OF FILMS 161

>   Ward Bond

568. THE OKLAHOMAN (1957)
     80m C
     D: Francis D. Lyon
     S: Joel McCrea
        Barbara Hale
        Brad Dexter
        Gloria Talbott
        Verna Felton
        Douglas Dick

569. OREGON PASSAGE (1957)
     82m C
     D: Paul Landres
     S: John Ericson
        Lola Albright
        Edward Platt
        Jon Shepodd

570. PAWNEE (1957)
     80m C
     D: George Waggner
     S: George Montgomery
        Bill Williams
        Lola Albright
        Francis J. McDonald
        Raymond Hatton

571. QUANTEZ (1957)
     80m C
     D: Harry Keller
     S: Fred MacMurray
        Dorothy Malone
        Sydney Chaplin
        John Gavin

572. REVOLT AT FORT LARAMIE (1957)
     73m C
     D: Lesley Selander
     S: John Dehner
        Frances Helm
        Gregg Palmer

            Don Gordon
            Robert Keys

573.   THE RIDE BACK (1957)
        79m B-W
        D: Allen H. Miner
        S: Anthony Quinn
            Lita Milan
            William Conrad
            Ellen Hope Monroe
            Louis Towers

574.   RIDE OUT FOR REVENGE (1957)
        79m B-W
        D: Bernard Girard
        S: Rory Calhoun
            Gloria Grahame
            Lloyd Bridges
            Vince Edwards

575.   RUN OF THE ARROW (1957)
        86m C
        D: Samuel Fuller
        S: Rod Steiger
            Brian Keith
            Sarita Montiel
            Ralph Meeker
            Charles Bronson
            Tim McCoy

576.   SHOOT OUT AT MEDICINE BEND (1957)
        87m B-W
        D: Richard L. Bare
        S: Randolph Scott
            James Craig
            Angie Dickinson
            Dani Crayne
            James Garner
            Gordon Jones

577.   TROOPER HOOK (1957)
        81m B-W
        D: Charles Marquis Warren

LIST OF FILMS 163

> S: Joel McCrea
> Barbara Stanwyck
> Earl Holliman
> Susan Kohner
> Sheb Wooley
> Celia Lovsky

578. WAR DRUMS (1957)
75m C
D: Reginald LeBorg
S: Lex Barker
Joan Taylor
Ben Johnson
Stuart Whitman

579. AMBUSH AT CIMARRON PASS (1958)
73m B-W
D: Jodie Copelan
S: Scott Brady
Margia Dean
Baynes Barron
William Vaughn

580. APACHE TERRITORY (1958)
75m C
D: Ray Nazarro
S: Rory Calhoun
Barbara Bates
John Dehner
Carolyn Craig

581. BADMAN'S COUNTRY (1958)
68m B-W
D: Fred F. Sears
S: George Montgomery
Buster Crabbe
Neville Brand
Malcolm Atterbury

582. BLOOD ARROW (1958)
75m B-W
D: Charles Marquis Warren
S: Scott Brady

Paul Richards
Phyllis Coates
Don Haggerty

583. THE BRAVADOS (1958)
98m C
D: Henry King
S: Gregory Peck
Joan Collins
Stephen Boyd
Albert Salmi

584. BULLWHIP (1958)
80m C
D: Harmon Jones
S: Guy Madison
Rhonda Fleming
James Griffith
Don Beddoe

585. COWBOY (1958)
92m C
D: Delmer Daves
S: Glenn Ford
Jack Lemmon
Anna Kashfi
Brian Donlevy
Dick York

586. ESCAPE FROM RED ROCK (1958)
75m B-W
D: Edward Bernds
S: Brian Donlevy
Jay C. Flippen
Eilene Janssen
Gary Murray

587. FLAMING FRONTIER (1958)
70m B-W
D: Sam Newfeld
S: Paisley Maxwell
Cecil Linder
Peter Humphreys

Ben Lennick

588. FORT DOBBS (1958)
    90m B-W
    D: Gordon Douglas
    S: Clint Walker
       Virginia Mayo
       Brian Keith
       Richard Eyer

589. FORT MASSACRE (1958)
    80m C
    D: Joseph M. Newman
    S: Joel McCrea
       Forrest Tucker
       Susan Cabot
       John Russell

590. FROM HELL TO TEXAS (1958)
    100m C
    D: Henry Hathaway
    S: Don Murray
       Diane Varsi
       Chill Wills
       Dennis Hopper

591. GUNMAN'S WALK (1958)
    97m C
    D: Phil Karlson
    S: Van Heflin
       Tab Hunter
       Kathryn Grant
       James Darren

592. THE LAW AND JAKE WADE (1958)
    86m C
    D: John Sturges
    S: Robert Taylor
       Richard Widmark
       Patricia Owens
       Robert Middleton

593. THE LIGHT IN THE FOREST (1958)

93m C
D: Herschel Daugherty
S: James MacArthur
   Carol Lynley
   Fess Parker
   Wendell Corey
   Joanne Dru
   Jessica Tandy
   Joseph Calleia
   John McIntire

594. THE LONE RANGER AND THE LOST CITY OF GOLD (1958)
80m C
D: Lesley Selander
S: Clayton Moore
   Jay Silverheels
   Douglas Kennedy
   Charles Watts

595. THE RAWHIDE TRAIL (1958)
67m B-W
D: Robert Gordon
S: Rex Reason
   Nancy Gates
   Richard Erdman
   Ann Doran

596. TONKA (1958)
97m C
D: Lewis R. Foster
S: Sal Mineo
   Philip Carey
   Jerome Courtland
   Rafael Campos
   H.M. Wynant
   Joy Page

597. ALIAS JESSE JAMES (1959)
92m C
D: Norman McLeod
S: Bob Hope
   Rhonda Fleming

LIST OF FILMS

      Wendell Corey
      Jim Davis
      Gloria Talbott

598. DAY OF THE OUTLAW (1959)
    91m B-W
    D: Andre de Toth
    S: Robert Ryan
       Burl Ives
       Tina Louise
       Alan Marshal
       Nehemiah Persoff
       Venetia Stevenson

599. ESCORT WEST (1959)
    75m B-W
    D: Francis D. Lyon
    S: Victor Mature
       Elaine Stewart
       Faith Domerque
       Reba Waters
       Noah Beery
       Leo Gordon
       Rex Ingram

600. THE FBI STORY (1959)
    149m C
    D: Mervyn LeRoy
    S: James Stewart
       Vera Miles
       Murray Hamilton
       Larry Pennell
       Nick Adams
       Diane Jergens
       Joyce Taylor

601. LAST TRAIN FROM GUN HILL (1959)
    94m C
    D: John Sturges
    S: Kirk Douglas
       Anthony Quinn
       Carolyn Jones
       Earl Holliman

        Brad Dexter
        Brian Hutton
        Ziva Rodann

602.　THE OREGON TRAIL (1959)
        86m C
        D: Gene Fowler, Jr.
        S: Fred MacMurray
           William Bishop
           Nina Shipman
           Gloria Talbott
           Henry Hull
           John Carradine

603.　RIDE LONESOME (1959)
        73m C
        D: Budd Boetticher
        S: Randolph Scott
           Karen Steele
           Pernell Roberts
           James Coburn
           Lee Van Cleef
           James Best

604.　THE SAVAGE INNOCENTS (1959)
        110m C
        D: Nicholas Ray
        S: Anthony Quinn
           Yoko Tan
           Peter O'Toole
           Marie Yang

605.　THE SHERIFF OF FRACTURED JAW (1959)
        103m C
        D: Raoul Walsh
        S: Kenneth More
           Jayne Mansfield
           Henry Hull
           William Campbell
           Bruce Cabot
           Robert Morley

606.　THUNDER IN THE SUN (1959)

LIST OF FILMS

      81m C
      D: Russell Rouse
      S: Susan Hayward
         Jeff Chandler
         Jacques Bergerac
         Blanche Yurka
         Carl Esmond
         Fortunio Bonanova

607. THE WILD AND THE INNOCENT (1959)
      84m C
      D: Jack Sher
      S: Audie Murphy
         Joanne Dru
         Gilbert Roland
         Jim Backus
         Sandra Dee
         George Mitchell
         Peter Breck

608. YELLOWSTONE KELLY (1959)
      91m C
      D: Gordon Douglas
      S: Clint Walker
         Edward Byrnes
         John Russell
         Ray Danton
         Claude Akins
         Rhodes Reason
         Warren Oates

1960-1969

609. ALL THE YOUNG MEN (1960)
      87m B-W
      D: Hall Bartlett
      S: Alan Ladd
         Sidney Poitier
         James Darren
         Glenn Corbett
         Mort Sahl

610. COMANCHE STATION (1960)
    74m C
    D: Budd Boetticher
    S: Randolph Scott
       Nancy Gates
       Claude Akins
       Skip Homeier

611. FLAMING STAR (1960)
    101m C
    D: Don Siegel
    S: Elvis Presley
       John McIntire
       Barbara Eden
       Steve Forrest
       Dolores Del Rio

612. FOR THE LOVE OF MIKE (1960)
    84m C
    D: George Sherman
    S: Richard Basehart
       Stuart Erwin
       Arthur Shields
       Armando Silvestre

613. OKLAHOMA TERRITORY (1960)
    67m B-W
    D: Edward L. Cahn
    S: Bill Williams
       Gloria Talbott
       Ted de Corsia
       Grant Richards
       Walter Sande

614. THE PLUNDERERS (1960)
    93m C
    D: Joseph Pevney
    S: Jeff Chandler
       John Saxon
       Dolores Hart
       Marsha Hunt
       Jay C. Flippen

615. SERGEANT RUTLEDGE (1960)
    118m C
    D: John Ford
    S: Jeffrey Hunter
       Constance Towers
       Billie Burke
       Woody Strode
       Juano Hernandez
       Willis Bouchey
       May Marsh

616. THE UNFORGIVEN (1960)
    125m C
    D: John Huston
    S: Burt Lancaster
       Audrey Hepburn
       Audie Murphy
       John Saxon
       Charles Bickford
       Lillian Gish

617. WALK TALL (1960)
    60m C
    D: Maury Dexter
    S: Willard Parker
       Joyce Meadows
       Kent Taylor

618. ALL HANDS ON DECK (1961)
    98m C
    D: Norman Taurog
    S: Pat Boone
       Buddy Hackett
       Dennis O'Keefe
       Barbara Eden

619. THE CANADIANS (1961)
    85m C
    D: Burt Kennedy
    S: Robert Ryan
       John Dehner
       Torin Thatcher
       John Sutton

Teresa Stratas

620. THE COMANCHEROS (1961)
 107m C
 D: Michael Curtiz
 S: John Wayne
  Stuart Whitman
  Lee Marvin
  Ina Balin
  Bruce Cabot
  Nehemiah Persoff

621. DAYS OF THRILLS AND LAUGHTER (1961)
 93m B-W
 Compiled by Robert Youngson
 S: Laurel and Hardy
  Charlie Chaplin
  Keystone Kops

622. THE DEADLY COMPANIONS (1961)
 90m C
 D: Sam Peckinpah
 S: Maureen O'Hara
  Brian Keith
  Steve Cochran
  Chill Wills

623. THE EXILES (1961)
 80m C
 D: Kent MacKenzie
 S: Yvonne Williams
  Homer Nish
  Tommy Reynolds

624. FRONTIER UPRISING (1961)
 68m B-W
 D: Edward L. Cahn
 S: James Davis
  Nancy Hadley
  Ken Mayer
  Nestor Paiva

625. THE OUTSIDER (1961)

LIST OF FILMS 173

>
> 108m B-W
> D: Delbert Mann
> S: Tony Curtis
>   James Franciscus
>   Bruce Bennett
>   Gregory Walcott
>   Vivian Nathan

626. POSSE FROM HELL (1961)
     89m C
     D: Herbert Coleman
     S: Audie Murphy
        John Saxon
        Zohra Lampert
        Vic Morrow
        Lee Van Cleef

627. THE PURPLE HILLS (1961)
     60m C
     D: Maury Dexter
     S: Gene Nelson
        Joanna Barnes
        Ken Taylor
        Russ Bender

628. A THUNDER OF DRUMS (1961)
     97m C
     D: Joseph M. Newman
     S: George Hamilton
        Luana Patten
        Richard Boone
        Charles Bronson
        Richard Chamberlain
        Slim Pickens

629. TWO RODE TOGETHER (1961)
     109m C
     D: John Ford
     S: James Stewart
        Richard Widmark
        Linda Cristal
        Shirley Jones
        Andy Devine

630. GERONIMO (1962)
 101m C
 D: Arnold Laven
 S: Chuck Connors
    Kamala Devi
    Ross Martin
    Adam West
    Pat Conway
    Larry Dobkin

631. SERGEANTS 3 (1962)
 112m C
 D: John Sturges
 S: Frank Sinatra
    Dean Martin
    Sammy Davis, Jr.
    Peter Lawford
    Joey Bishop

632. SEVEN SEAS TO CALAIS (1962)
 102m C
 D: Rudolph Mate
 S: Primo Zeglio
    Rod Taylor
    Keith Michell
    Irene Worth

633. SIX BLACK HORSES (1962)
 80m C
 D: Harry Keller
 S: Audie Murphy
    Dan Duryea
    Joan O'Brien
    George Wallace

634. STAGECOACH TO DANCER'S ROCK (1962)
 72m B-W
 D: Earl Bellamy
 S: Warren Stevens
    Martin Landau
    Jody Lawrence
    Judy Dan

LIST OF FILMS 175

635. THE WILD WESTERNERS (1962)
 70m C
 D: Oscar Rudolph
 S: James Philbrook
    Nancy Kovack
    Duane Eddy
    Guy Mitchell

636. YOUNG GUNS OF TEXAS (1962)
 78m C
 D: Maury Dexter
 S: James Mitchum
    Alana Ladd
    Jody McCrea
    Chill Wills

637. BLACK GOLD (1963)
 98m B-W
 D: Leslie Martinson
 S: Philip Carey
    Diane McBain
    James Best
    Claude Akins
    Iron Eyes Cody

638. HOW THE WEST WAS WON (1963)
 155m C
 D: John Ford
    Henry Hathaway
    George Marshall
 S: George Peppard
    Debbie Reynolds
    Carroll Baker
    James Stewart
    Henry Fonda
    John Wayne
    Gregory Peck

639. KINGS OF THE SUN (1963)
 108m C
 D: J. Lee Thompson
 S: Yul Brynner
    George Chakiris

Shirley Ann Field
Richard Basehart
Brad Dexter

640. MCLINTOCK (1963)
     127m C
     D: Andrew V. McLaglen
     S: John Wayne
        Maureen O'Hara
        Patrick Wayne
        Stefanie Powers
        Yvonne DeCarlo
        Chill Wills
        Bruce Cabot

641. THE RAIDERS (1963)
     75m C
     D: Herschel Daugherty
     S: Robert Culp
        Brian Keith
        Judi Meredith
        James McMullan
        Alfred Ryder
        Simon Oakland

642. SAVAGE SAM (1963)
     103m C
     D: Norman Tokar
     S: Brian Keith
        Tommy Kirk
        Kevin Corcoran
        Dewey Martin
        Jeff York

643. APACHE RIFLES (1964)
     92m C
     D: William Witney
     S: Audie Murphy
        Michael Dante
        Linda Lawson
        John Archer
        J. Pat O'Malley

LIST OF FILMS 177

644. BLOOD ON THE ARROW (1964)
      91m C
      D: Sidney Salkow
      S: Dale Robertson
         Martha Hyer
         Wendell Corey
         Elisha Cook
         Ted de Corsia

645. BULLET FOR A BADMAN (1964)
      80m C
      D: R.G. Springsteen
      S: Audie Murphy
         Darren McGavin
         Ruta Lee
         Skip Homeier
         George Tobias
         Bob Steele

646. CHEYENNE AUTUMN (1964)
      160m C
      D: John Ford
      S: Carroll Baker
         Richard Widmark
         Edward G. Robinson
         Dolores Del Rio
         Ricardo Montalban
         Gilbert Roland
         Sal Mineo
         Victor Jory

647. A DISTANT TRUMPET (1964)
      117m C
      D: Raoul Walsh
      S: Troy Donahue
         Suzanne Pleshette
         Kent Smith
         Claude Akins
         James Gregory

648. HE RIDES TALL (1964)
      84m B-W
      D: R.G. Springsteen

S: Tony Young
Dan Duryea
Madlyn Rhue
George Petrie

649. MAN'S FAVORITE SPORT? (1964)
120m C
D: Howard Hawks
S: Rock Hudson
Paula Prentiss
John McGiver
Maria Perschy
Roscoe Karns

650. RIO CONCHOS (1964)
107m C
D: Gordon Douglas
S: Richard Boone
Stuart Whitman
Tony Franciosa
Edmond O'Brien

651. STAGE TO THUNDER ROCK (1964)
82m C
D: William F. Claxon
S: Barry Sullivan
Marilyn Maxwell
Lon Chaney
Scott Brady
John Agar
Keenan Wynn

652. TAGGART (1964)
85m C
D: R.G. Springsteen
S: Tony Young
Dan Duryea
Peter Duryea
David Carradine
Jean Hale
Harry Carey
Bob Steele

LIST OF FILMS 179

653. APACHE GOLD (1965)
    91m C
    D: Harold Reinl
    S: Lex Barker
       Mario Adorf
       Pierre Brice
       Marie Versini

654. CAT BALLOU (1965)
    96m C
    D: Elliott Silverstein
    S: Jane Fonda
       Lee Marvin
       Nat King Cole
       Michael Callan
       Dwayne Hickman
       Reginald Denny
       Jay C. Flippen

655. FINGER ON THE TRIGGER (1965)
    87m C
    D: Sidney Pink
    S: Rory Calhoun
       James Philbrook
       Todd Martin
       Silvia Solar
       Brad Talbot

656. THE GLORY GUYS (1965)
    112m C
    D: Arnold Laven
    S: Tom Tryon
       Harve Presnell
       Michael Anderson, Jr.
       Senta Berger
       James Caan
       Slim Pickens

657. THE GREAT SIOUX MASSACRE (1965)
    91m C
    D: Sidney Salkow
    S: Joseph Cotten
       Darren McGavin

Philip Carey
Julie Sommars
Nancy Kovack
John Matthews
Frank Ferguson

658. THE HALLELUJAH TRAIL (1965)
 165m C
 D: John Sturges
 S: Burt Lancaster
    Lee Remick
    Jim Hutton
    Brian Keith
    Martin Landau
    Donald Pleasence

659. MAJOR DUNDEE (1965)
 124m C
 D: Sam Peckinpah
 S: Charlton Heston
    Richard Harris
    Jim Hutton
    James Coburn
    Michael Anderson, Jr.
    Senta Berger
    Warren Oates
    Slim Pickens

660. THE TREASURE OF SILVER LAKE (1965)
 88m C
 D: Harold Reinl
 S: Lex Barker
    Gotz George
    Pierre Brice
    Herbert Lom
    Karin Dor
    Marianne Hoppe

661. APACHE UPRISING (1966)
 90m C
 D: R.G. Springsteen
 S: Rory Calhoun
    Corinne Calvet

John Russell
Lon Chaney
Gene Evans
Richard Arlen
Arthur Hunnicutt
Johnny Mack Brown
Jean Parker

662. DUEL AT DIABLO (1966)
103m C
D: Ralph Nelson
S: James Garner
Sidney Poitier
Bibi Anderson
Dennis Weaver
Bill Travers

663. 40 GUNS TO APACHE PASS (1966)
95m C
D: William Witney
S: Audie Murphy
Michael Burns
Kenneth Tobey
Laraine Stephens
Michael Blodgett
Michael Keep

664. FRONTIER HELLCAT (1966)
98m C
D: Alfred Vohrer
S: Stewart Granger
Elke Sommer
Pierre Brice
Gotz George

665. INCIDENT AT PHANTOM HILL (1966)
88m C
D: Earl Bellamy
S: Robert Fuller
Dan Duryea
Jocelyn Lane
Claude Akins

666. JOHNNY TIGER (1966)
    102m C
    D: Paul Wendkos
    S: Robert Taylor
       Geraldine Brooks
       Chad Everett
       Brenda Scott

667. KID RODELO (1966)
    91m B-W
    D: Richard Carlson
    S: Don Murray
       Janet Leigh
       Broderick Crawford
       Richard Carlson

668. NAVAJO JOE (1966)
    89m C
    D: Sergio Corbucci
    S: Burt Reynolds
       Aldo San Brell
       Tanya Lopert
       Fernando Rey

669. NEVADA SMITH (1966)
    135m C
    D: Henry Hathaway
    S: Steve McQueen
       Karl Malden
       Brian Keith
       Arthur Kennedy
       Suzanne Pleshette
       Raf Vallone
       Pat Hingle

670. THE PLAINSMAN (1966)
    92m C
    D: David Lowell Rich
    S: Don Murray
       Guy Stockwell
       Abby Dalton
       Bradford Dillman
       Lesley Nielsen

LIST OF FILMS 183

671. RAMPAGE AT APACHE WELLS (1966)
 90m C
 D: Harold Philipps
 S: Stewart Granger
    Pierre Brice
    Macha Meril
    Harold Leipnitz

672. STAGECOACH (1966)
 115m C
 D: Gordon Douglas
 S: Ann-Margaret
    Alex Cord
    Red Buttons
    Michael Connors
    Bing Crosby
    Bob Cummings
    Van Heflin
    Slim Pickens
    Stephanie Powers
    Keenan Wynn

673. THE TALL WOMEN (1966)
 101m C
 D: Sidney Pink
 S: Anne Baxter
    Maria Perschy
    Rosella Como
    John Clarke

674. TEXAS ACROSS THE RIVER (1966)
 101m C
 D: Michael Gordon
 S: Dean Martin
    Alain Delon
    Joey Bishop
    Rosemary Forsyth
    Peter Graves
    Tina Marquand

675. CHUCKA (1967)
 105m C
 D: Gordon Douglas

S: Rod Taylor
John Mills
Ernest Borgnine
Luciana Paluzzi
James Whitmore
Angela Dorian
Louis Hayward

676. HOMBRE (1967)
111m C
D: Martin Ritt
S: Paul Newman
Fredric March
Richard Boone
Diane Cilento
Cameron Mitchell
Barbara Rush
Martin Balsam

677. RED TOMAHAWK (1967)
82m C
D: R.G. Springsteen
S: Howard Keel
Joan Caulfield
Broderick Crawford
Scott Brady
Wendell Corey
Richard Arlen
Tom Drake
Ben Cooper
Donald Barry

678. THE WAR WAGON (1967)
101m C
D: Burt Kennedy
S: John Wayne
Kirk Douglas
Howard Keel
Robert Walker
Keenan Wynn
Bruce Cabot
Joanna Barnes

LIST OF FILMS 185

679. THE WAY WEST (1967)
    122m C
    D: Andrew V. McLaglen
    S: Kirk Douglas
       Robert Mitchum
       Richard Widmark
       Lola Albright
       Michael Witney
       Stubby Kaye
       Sally Field

680. CUSTER OF THE WEST (1968)
    140m C
    D: Robert Siodmak
    S: Robert Shaw
       Mary Ure
       Jeffrey Hunter
       Robert Ryan
       Ty Hardin
       Charles Stalnaker

681. DAY OF THE EVIL GUN (1968)
    93m C
    D: Jerry Thorpe
    S: Glen Ford
       Arthur Kennedy
       Dean Jagger
       John Anderson
       Paul Fix
       Nino Minardos
       Royal Dano

682. THE FASTEST GUITAR ALIVE (1968)
    87m C
    D: Michael Moore
    S: Roy Orbison
       Sammy Jackson
       Maggie Pierce
       Joan Freeman

683. FORT UTAH (1968)
    83m C
    D: Lesley Selander

S: John Ireland
    Virginia Mayo
    Scott Brady
    John Russell
    Robert Strauss
    James Craig
    Richard Arlen
    Jim Davis

684. THE SAVAGE SEVEN (1968)
     96m C
     D: Richard Rush
     S: Robert Walker
        Larry Bishop
        Adam Roarke
        Max Julien
        Duane Eddy

685. THE SCALPHUNTERS (1968)
     102m C
     D: Sydney Pollack
     S: Burt Lancaster
        Shelley Winters
        Ossie Davis
        Telly Savalas
        Armando Silvestre
        Dabney Coleman

686. THE SHAKIEST GUN IN THE WEST (1968)
     101m C
     D: Alan Rafkin
     S: Don Knotts
        Barbara Rhoades
        Jackie Coogan
        Donald Barry
        Ruth McDevitt
        Frank McGrath

687. SHALAKO (1968)
     113m C
     D: Edward Dmytryk
     S: Sean Connery
        Brigitte Bardot

LIST OF FILMS 187

        Stephen Boyd
        Jack Hawkins
        Peter van Eyck
        Honor Blackman

688. STAY AWAY, JOE (1968)
    102m C
    D: Peter Tweksbury
    S: Elvis Presley
       Burgess Meredith
       Joan Blondell
       Katy Jurado
       Thomas Gomez
       Henry Jones

689. WHITE COMANCHE (1968)
    90m C
    D: Gilbert Kay (Jose Briz)
    S: Joseph Cotten
       William Shatner
       Perla Cristal
       Rossana Yanni

690. HEAVEN WITH A GUN (1969)
    101m C
    D: Lee H. Katzin
    S: Glenn Ford
       Carolyn Jones
       Barbara Hershey
       John Anderson
       David Carradine

691. MCKENNA'S GOLD (1969)
    128m C
    D: J. Lee Thompson
    S: Gregory Peck
       Omar Sharif
       Telly Savalas
       Camilla Sparv
       Keenan Wynn
       Julie Newmar
       Lee J. Cobb
       Raymond Massey

          Burgess Meredith

692. THE STALKING MOON (1969)
      109m C
      D: Robert Mulligan
      S: Gregory Peck
         Eva Marie Saint
         Robert Forster
         Noland Clay
         Russell Thorson
         Frank Silvera

693. TELL THEM WILLIE BOY IS HERE (1969)
      96m C
      D: Abraham Polonsky
      S: Robert Redford
         Katharine Ross
         Robert Blake
         Susan Clark
         Barry Sullivan

                    1970-1979

694. FLAP (1970)
      106m C
      D: Carol Reed
      S: Anthony Quinn
         Claude Akins
         Tony Bill
         Victor Jory
         Shelley Winters

695. LAND RAIDERS (1970)
      100m C
      D: Nathan Juran
      S: Telly Savalas
         George Maharis
         Arlene Dahl
         Janet Landgard
         Jocelyn Lane
         George Coulouris

LIST OF FILMS 189

      Guy Rolfe

696. LITTLE BIG MAN (1970)
    150m C
    D: Arthur Penn
    S: Dustin Hoffman
       Faye Dunaway
       Martin Balsam
       Richard Mulligan
       Chief Dan George
       Jeff Corey
       Amy Eccles

697. A MAN CALLED HORSE (1970)
    114m C
    D: Elliott Silverstein
    S: Richard Harris
       Judith Anderson
       Jean Gascon
       Manu Tupou
       Corinna Tsopei
       Dub Taylor

698. THE MCMASTERS (1970)
    97m C
    D: Alf Kjellin
    S: Burl Ives
       Brock Peters
       David Carradine
       Nancy Kwan
       Jack Palance
       John Carradine

699. RUN, SIMON, RUN (1970)
    73m C
    D: George McCowan
    S: Burt Reynolds
       Inger Stevens
       Royal Dano
       James Best
       Rodolfo Acosta
       Don Dubbins
       Ken Lynch

700. SABATA (1970)
    107m C
    D: Frank Kramer (Gianfranco Parolini)
    S; Lee Van Cleef
       William Berger
       Franco Ressel
       Linda Veras
       Pedro Sanchez (Ignazio Spalla)

701. SOLDIER BLUE (1970)
    112m C
    D: Ralph Nelson
    S: Candice Bergen
       Peter Straus
       Donald Pleasence
       John Anderson
       Jorge Rivero
       Dana Elcar

702. WILD WOMEN (1970)
    73m C
    D: Don Taylor
    S: Hugh O'Brian
       Anne Francis
       Marilyn Maxwell
       Marie Windsor
       Sherry Jackson
       Cynthia Hull

703. BILLY JACK (1972)
    112m C
    D: T.C. Frank (Tom Laughlin)
    S: Tom Laughlin
       Delores Hart
       Clark Howett
       Bert Freed
       Julie Webb

704. HOUSE MADE OF DAWN (1972)
    91m C
    D: Richardson Morse
    S: John Saxon
       Larry Littlebird

LIST OF FILMS   191

705. JEREMIAH JOHNSON (1972)
      107m C
      D: Sydney Pollack
      S: Robert Redford
          Will Geer
          Stefan Gierasch
          Allyn Ann McLerie
          Charles Tyner
          Josh Albee

706. ULZANA'S RAID (1972)
      103m C
      D: Robert Aldrich
      S: Bert Lancaster
          Bruce Davison
          Jorge Luke
          Richard Jaeckel
          Joaquin Martinez
          Lloyd Bochner
          Karl Swenson

707. WHEN THE LEGENDS DIE (1972)
      105m C
      D: Stuart Millar
      S: Richard Widmark
          Frederic Forrest
          Luana Anders
          Vito Scotti
          Herbert Nelson

708. TRIAL OF BILLY JACK (1974)
      170m C
      D: Frank (Tom) Laughlin
      S: Tom Laughlin
          Delores Taylor
          Victor Izay
          Teresa Laughlin
          William Wellman, Jr.
          Russell Lane
          Michell Wilson

709. WHITE DAWN (1974)
      109m C

D: Philip Kaufman
S: Warren Oates
   Timothy Bottoms
   Lou Gossett
   Simonie Kopapik
   Joanasie Salominie
   Pilitak
   Sagiaktok
   Munamee Sake
   Pitseolala Kih

710. ONE FLEW OVER THE CUCKOO'S NEST (1975)
     129m C
     D: Milos Forman
     S: Jack Nicholson
        Louise Fletcher
        William Redfield
        Michael Beryman
        Brad Dourif
        Peter Brocco
        Will Sampson

711. BUFFALO BILL AND THE INDIANS (1976)
     120m C
     D: Robert Altman
     S: Paul Newman
        Burt Lancaster
        Will Sampson
        Joel Gray
        Geraldine Chaplin
        Kevin McCarthy

712. THE OUTLAW JOSEY WALES (1976)
     135m C
     D: Clint Eastwood
     S: Clint Eastwood
        Chief Dan George
        Sondra Locke
        Bill McKinney
        John Vernon
        Paula Trueman
        Sam Bottoms
        Geraldine Keams

LIST OF FILMS

713. RETURN OF A MAN CALLED HORSE (1976)
     125m C
     D: Irvin Kershner
     S: Richard Harris
        Gale Sondergaard
        Geoffrey Lewis
        Bill Lucking
        Jorge Luke

714. WINTERHAWK (1976)
     98m C
     D: Charles B. Pierce
     S: Leif Erickson
        Woody Strode
        Denver Pyle
        L.W. Jones
        Michael Dante

715. THE LAST OF THE MOHICANS (1977)
     100m C (TVM)
     D: James L. Conway
     S: Steve Forrest
        Ned Romero
        Andrew Prine
        Robert Tessier
        Don Shanks
        Jane Actman

716. MANITOU (1977)
     105m C
     D: William Girdler
     S: Tony Curtis
        Michael Ansara
        Susan Strassberg
        Stella Stevens
        Ann Southern
        Burgess Meredith

717. THE WHITE BUFFALO (1977)
     97m C
     D: J. Lee Thompson
     S: Charles Bronson
        Jack Warden

Will Sampson
Kim Novak
Clint Walker

718. THREE WARRIORS (1978)
105m C
D: Keith Merrill
S: Charles White Eagle
Lois Red Elk
McKee "Kiko" Red Wing
Christopher Lloyd
Randy Quaid

719. EAGLE'S WING (1979)
104m C
D: Anthony Harvey
S: Martin Sheen
Sam Waterston
Harvey Keitel
Stephane Audran
Caroline Langrishe

720. NIGHTWING (1979)
103m C
D: Arthur Miller
S: Nick Mancuso
David Warner
Kathryn Harrold
Stephen Macht
Strother Martin

1980-1982

721. THE MOUNTAIN MEN (1980)
102m C
D: Richard Lang
S: Charlton Heston
Brian Keith
Victoria Racimo
Stephen Macht
John Glover

LIST OF FILMS

722. COMIN' AT YA (1981)
    91m C (3-D)
    D: Ferdinando Baldi
    S: Tony Anthony
       Gene Quintana
       Victoria Abril
       Ricardo Palacios
       Gordon Lewis

723. THE LEGEND OF THE LONE RANGER (1981)
    98m C
    D: William A. Fraker
    S: Klinton Spilsbury
       Michael Horse
       Christopher Lloyd
       Matt Clark
       Juanin Clay

724. WINDWALKER (1981)
    108m C
    D: Keith Merrill
    S: Trevor Howard
       Nick Ramus
       James Remar
       Serene Hedin
       Dusty Iron Wing McCrea
       Silvana Gallardo
       Bill Drago
       Rudy Diaz
       Harold Goss Coyote
       Roy Cohoe
       Jason Stevens
       Emerson John
       Marvin Takes Horse

725. TRIUMPHS OF A MAN CALLED HORSE III (1982)
    91m C
    D: John Hough
    S: Richard Harris
       Michael Beck
       Ana de Sade

Index

Index

Abenaki 203
Access 153
ACROSS THE WIDE MISSOURI 443
Adair, John 192
Agabiti, Thomas 225
Ahab, Captain 287
Aitken, Will 60
Aldrich, Robert 302, 347, 497, 706
Alexander, Shana 226
ALIAS JESSE JAMES 597
ALLEGHENY UPRISING 380
Allen, Irving 456
Allen, T. 227
ALL HANDS ON DECK 618
ALL THE YOUNG MEN 609
Altman, Robert 60, 195, 230, 304, 311, 322, 333, 339, 341, 349, 361, 711
AMBUSH 418
AMBUSH AT CIMARRON PASS 579
AMBUSH AT TOMAHAWK GAP 478
AMERICA 151
AMERICAN FILM HERITAGE, THE 346
AMERICAN HISTORY/AMERICAN FILM: INTERPRETING THE HOLLYWOOD IMAGE 152
American Horse, George 175
AMERICAN INDIAN IN SHORT FICTION, THE: AN ANNOTATED BIBLIOGRAPHY 5
American Indian Movement 116
AMERICAN WEST ON FILM, THE: MYTH AND REALITY 141
Ames, Katrine 61
Anderson, Michael 544
ANNIE GET YOUR GUN 427
ANNIE OAKLEY 371
Apache 54, 128, 342
APACHE 238, 284, 302, 497
APACHE AMBUSH 522
APACHE DRUMS 444
APACHE GOLD 653
APACHE RIFLES 643
APACHE TERRITORY 580
APACHE UPRISING 661
APACHE WARRIOR 565
APACHE WAR SMOKE 462
Arapahoe 174
Archainbaud, George 404
AROUND THE WORLD IN 80 DAYS 544
ARROWHEAD 479
ARROW IN THE DUST 498
Astor, Gerald 228

Aztec 189

BACKLASH 545
Bacon, Lloyd 487
BAD BASCOMB 398
BADLANDS OF DAKOTA 391
BADMAN'S COUNTRY 581
BADMAN'S TERRITORY 399
Baldi, Ferdinando 722
BALLAD OF CROWFOOT, THE 85, 111
Balshofer, Fred J. 62
Bare, Richard L. 576
Barnett, Louise K. 2
Barry, Roxana 3
Bartlett, Hall 609
Bataille, Gretchen M. 4, 63, 64, 65, 66, 67, 169
BATTLE AT APACHE PASS, THE 463
BATTLE CRY 523
Battle of Little Big Horn 165
BATTLE OF ROGUE RIVER, THE 499
Battle of Wounded Knee 144
Beale, Lewis 68
Beaudine, William 403, 563
BEHIND THE SCENES: EQUAL EMPLOYMENT OPPORTUNITY IN THE MOTION PICTURE INDUSTRY 78
Beidler, Peter G. 5
Bell, Arthur 229
Bellamy, Earl 536, 634, 665
BEND OF THE RIVER 464
Bennett, Spencer G. 466
Bergen, Candace 205, 277
Berger, Thomas 362
Berkhofer, Robert F., Jr. 6
Bernds, Edward 586
Berstein, Gene M. 230
BIG SKY, THE 465
BIG TRAIL, THE 365
BILLY JACK 132, 197, 231, 235, 242, 301, 316, 363, 703
BIOGRAPH BULLETINS: 1896-1908 150
BLACK DAKOTAS, THE 500
BLACK GOLD 637
Black, Nancy B. 7
Blair, George 541
Blakey, Carla M. 69, 70
Blaustein, Julien 342
BLOOD ARROW 582
BLOOD ON THE ARROW 644
BLOOD ON THE MOON 408
Boetticher, Budd 492, 603, 610
BOWERY BUCKAROOS 403
Boyd, David 71
Boyd, George N. 231
Brando, Marlon 53, 54
Brascoupe, Simon 72
Braudy, Leo 232
Brauer, Donna 73
Brauer, Ralph 73
BRAVADOS, THE 583
BRAVE WARRIOR 466
Briz, Jose (Gilbert Kay) 689
BROKEN ARROW 118, 138, 151, 179, 198, 199, 200, 267, 283, 291, 318, 342, 428
BROKEN LANCE 501
BROKEN TREATY AT BATTLE MOUNTAIN 303
Brooks, Richard 551
Browne, Nicholas 233
Brownlow, Kevin 74

INDEX

Brudnoy, David 234
Bryon, Stuart 235
Buckley, Peter 236
Buckley, Tom 237
Bucklin, Louise L. 238
Budeley, Michael 239
Buffalo Bill 3, 32, 144, 201, 230, 315, 343
BUFFALO BILL 88, 201, 285, 397
BUFFALO BILL AND THE INDIANS 60, 61, 190, 195, 207, 227, 230, 249, 271, 272, 292, 304, 311, 315, 317, 322, 326, 333, 339, 341, 343, 348, 349, 361, 711
BUFFALO BILL AND THE WILD WEST 38
Buffalo Bill's Wild West Show 80, 304
BUGLES IN THE AFTERNOON 467
BULLET FOR A BADMAN 645
BULLWHIP 584
Bureau of Indian Affairs 174
Burgess, John Andrew 240
Bush, W. Stephen 75
Butler, David 503
Buzzell, Edward 386
Byler, Mary Gloyne 8

Cahn, Edward L. 613, 624
Calder, Jenni 76
Calder-Marshall, Arthur 77
California Advisory Committee to the U.S. Commission on Civil Rights 78

Callenbach, Ernest 241
CALL HER SAVAGE 368
CAMERAS WEST 137
CANADIAN PACIFIC 419
CANADIANS, THE 619
Canby, Vincent 242, 243, 244, 245
CANYON PASSAGE 400
CANYON RIVER 546
CAPTAIN JOHN SMITH AND POCAHONTAS 480
CARIBOO TRAIL, THE 429
Carlson, Richard 507, 667
Carol Burnett Show 135
Carpenter, Edmund 79
Castle, William 483, 485, 499, 509, 529
CAT BALLOU 654
CATTLE QUEEN OF MONTANA 502
CAVALRY SCOUT 445
Cawelti, John G. 80, 81, 82
CHARGE AT FEATHER RIVER, THE 481
Chavers, Dean 246
Cheyenne 174, 191, 202, 209, 297, 320, 323, 360
CHEYENNE AUTUMN 101, 118, 127, 151, 170, 191, 202, 209, 268, 273, 308, 314, 331, 335, 646
CHEYENNE RAIDERS 210
Chief Bromden 133
CHIEF CRAZY HORSE 524
Chippewa 57
CHUCKA 675
Churchill, Ward 83, 84
CIRCLE OF THE SUN 183
Clandfield, David 247

Clark, Joan 85
Claxon, William F. 651
Cline, Edward 388
Clum, John Philip 289, 355
Cochise 199
Cocks, Jay 248
Cody, William F. 311
Coen, Rena Neumann 9
Coleman, Herbert 626
Coleman, John 249, 250, 251
Collins, Lewis D. 469
Colonel Thursday 161
COLORADO TERRITORY 420
COLUMN SOUTH 482
Comanche 71
COMANCHE 547
COMANCHEROS, THE 620
COMANCHE STATION 610
COMANCHE TERRITORY 430
Combs, Richard 252, 253
COMIN' AT YA 722
COMMAND, THE 503
COMMON MISCONCEPTIONS ABOUT AMERICAN INDIANS 1
CONQUEST OF COCHISE 483
Constible, J.P. 254
Conway, James L. 715
Cooper, Arthur 255, 256
Corbucci, Sergio 668
Corliss, Richard 86
Costo, Jeannette 1
Costo, Rupert 10
COVERED WAGON, THE 350
COWBOY 585
Crabb, Jack 232
Crazy Horse 61
Creek 61, 133
Crist, Judith 257, 258
Crosland, Alan 370

Crow 300, 320
Cunningham, James P. 259
Curtis, Edward S. 21, 25
Curtiz, Michael 449, 620
Custer, George Armstrong 119, 161, 214, 221, 266
CUSTER OF THE WEST 680
CUSTER'S LAST FIGHT 145

DAKOTA INCIDENT 548
DANGEROUS MISSION 504
DANIEL BOONE, TRAIL BLAZER 549
Daugherty, Herschel 593, 641
Daves, Delmer 428, 505, 552, 585
DAVY CROCKETT--INDIAN SCOUT 431
DAVY CROCKETT, KING OF THE WILD FRONTIER 525
DAY OF THE EVIL GUN 681
DAY OF THE OUTLAW 598
DAYS OF THRILLS AND LAUGHTER 621
DEADLY COMPANIONS, THE 622
de Cordova, Frederick 482
DEFEATHERING THE INDIAN 23
Deloria, Vine, Jr. 25, 67, 141
DeMille, Cecil B. 367, 373, 385, 389, 407
deMontigny, Lionel H. 260
Denby, David 261
Dench, Ernest Alfred 87
Denton, James F. 88
Dervin, Daniel A. 89
de Toth, Andre 471, 530,

INDEX

de Toth, Andre (cont'd) 598
DEVIL'S DOORWAY 143, 151, 282, 286, 432
Dexter, Maury 617, 627, 636
Dieterle, William 455
Dillon, John Francis 368
DIME NOVEL WESTERN, THE 121
DiMino, Angelo V. 90
DISTANT DRUMS 446
DISTANT TRUMPET, A 647
Dmytryk, Edward 501, 687
Dodi, Steve 91
Douglas, Gordon 454, 481, 588, 608, 650, 672, 675
DRAGON WELLS MASSACRE 566
Drinnon, Richard 11
DRUM BEAT 505
DRUMS ACROSS THE RIVER 506
DRUMS ALONG THE MOHAWK 151, 152, 381
Ducheneaux, Franklin 12
DUDE GOES WEST, THE 409
DUEL AT DIABLO 662
DUEL IN THE SUN 401
Dwan, Allan 406, 502
D.W. GRIFFITH: THE YEARS AT BIOGRAPH 117

EACH MAN IN HIS TIME 359
EAGLE'S WING 719
Eder, Richard 262
Edwards, Ethan 319, 325
Egge, Marion F. 5
Eiselein, E.B. 92
Elrod, Norman 93
Emmens, Carol A. 94
END OF THE TRAIL, THE 85
Enright, Ray 447
Erens, Patricia 95, 263
ESCAPE FROM FORT BRAVO 484
ESCAPE FROM RED ROCK 586
ESCORT WEST 599
Eskimo 220
Esselman, Katherine 147
Everett, D.S. 727
Everson, William K. 96, 97, 100
Ewers, John C. 13, 14
EXILES, THE 129, 623
Eyles, Allen 98

FACING WEST: THE METAPHYSICS OF INDIAN-HATING AND EMPIRE BUILDING 11, 167
Farber, Stephen 264, 265
FAR HORIZONS, THE 526
Farrow, John 488
FASTEST GUITAR ALIVE, THE 682
FBI STORY, THE 600
Fenin, George N. 99, 100
FILMING OF THE WEST, THE 179
FILMS ON INDIANS AND INUIT OF NORTH AMERICA, 1965-1978 164
FINGER ON THE TRIGGER 655
Flaherty, Robert 77, 91
FLAMING FEATHER 447
FLAMING FRONTIER 587
FLAMING STAR 611
FLAP 159, 265, 305, 312, 353, 694
Florence, William R. 101
FOCUS ON THE WESTERN 147

Folsom, James K. 102
FOR THE LOVE OF MIKE 612
Ford, John 71, 98, 101, 125, 127, 130, 155, 156, 161, 170, 191, 202, 268, 273, 297, 308, 310, 314, 319, 331, 335, 351, 381, 383, 410, 425, 435, 440, 559, 615, 629, 638, 646
Forman, Milos 710
FORT APACHE 155, 161, 179, 191, 196, 293, 410
FORT DEFIANCE 448
FORT DOBBS 588
FORT MASSACRE 589
FORT OSAGE 468
FORT TI 485
FORT UTAH 683
FORT VENGEANCE 486
FORT YUMA 527
40 GUNS TO APACHE PASS 663
Foster, Lewis R. 450, 548, 596
Foster, Norman 414, 525
FOUR GUNS TO THE BORDER 507
Fowler, Gene, Jr. 602
FOXFIRE 528
Fraker, William A. 723
FRANK, T.C. (Tom Laughlin) 703
Franklin, Eliza 103
Freedman, Joel 303
Fregonese, Hugo 444
French, Philip 104, 105, 106, 266
Friar, Natasha A. 108
Friar, Ralph E. 107, 108
Friedman, Seymour 560
FROM HELL TO TEXAS 590
FRONTIER HELLCAT 664

FRONTIER UPRISING 624
Fuller, Samuel 225, 575
FURY AT FURNACE CREEK 411

Gannaway, Albert C. 549
GARDEN OF EVIL 508
Georgakas, Dan 109, 155
George, Chief Dan 215, 274, 299, 364
Gerdts, W.H. 15
Geronimo 284
GERONIMO (1939) 382
GERONIMO (1962) 141, 630
GERONIMO JONES 111
Gessner, Robert 267
Gillett, John 268
Gilliatt, Penelope 269, 270, 271
Girard, Bernard 574
Girdler, William 716
Glasrud, Bruce A. 16
GLORY GUYS, THE 656
Glut, Donald F. 112
GOLDEN WEST, THE 369
GO WEST 386
Goodman, Ezra 110
Gordon, Michael 674
Gordon, Robert 595
Gow, Gordon 272, 273, 274, 275, 276
Graham, Don 155
GREAT DAY IN THE MORNING 550
GREAT MOVIE SERIALS, THE: THEIR SOUND AND FURY 112
GREAT SIOUX MASSACRE, THE 657
GREAT SIOUX UPRISING, THE 487
GREAT TRAIN ROBBERY, THE 122

Green, Alfred E. 391
Greenspan, Roger 277
Griffith, D.W. 117, 184
Gross, Larry 278
GUNMAN'S WALK 591
GUN THAT WON THE WEST, THE 529
Gustkey, Earl 279

HALF-BLOOD, THE: A CULTURAL SYMBOL IN 19TH CENTURY AMERICAN FICTION 35, 167
HALF-BREED, THE 469
Hall, Mordaunt 280
HALLELUJAH TRAIL, THE 658
HALLIDAY BRAND 567
HANDBOOK OF NORTH AMERICAN INDIANS 139
Handelman, Janet 111
Handzo, Stephen 281, 282
Harmon, Jim 112
Harrington, John 113
Harris, Helen L. 114
Harris, Richard 248
Harrison, Louis Reeves 115
Hartman, Hedy 116
Hartung, Philip T. 283, 284, 285, 286, 287, 288, 289
Harvey, Anthony 719
Haskin, Bryon 459
Haspiel, James Robert 290
Hastings, Phyllis R. 160
Hatch, Robert 291, 292, 293, 294
Hathaway, Henry 395, 508, 590, 669
HAWK OF THE WILDERNESS 379

Hawks, Howard 415, 465, 649
Haycox, Ernest 247
HEAVEN WITH A GUN 690
Heisler, Stuart 426, 553
Henderson, Robert M. 117
Henry, Jeannette 10
HE RIDES TALL 648
HEROES, HEAVIES AND SAGEBRUSH: A PICTORIAL HISTORY OF THE "B" WESTERN PLAYERS 136
Hibbs, Jesse 562
Hill, Mary Ann 84
Hill, Norbert 84
Hill, Richard 118
Hoffman, Dustin 228, 364
HOLLYWOOD INDIAN, THE: STEREOTYPES OF NATIVE AMERICANS IN FILMS 151
HOLLYWOOD: THE GOLDEN ERA 172
HOMBRE 264, 676
HONDO 179, 488
Hopper, Jerry 491
HORIZONS WEST: STUDIES IN AUTHORSHIP IN THE WESTERN FILM 128
Horne, James W. 377
HORSE, THE GUN, AND THE PIECE OF PROPERTY, THE: CHANGING IMAGES OF THE TV WESTERN 73
Hough, John 725
HOUSE MADE OF DAWN 63, 118, 704
HOUSE OF BEADLE AND ADAMS, THE 20
HOW THE WEST WAS WON 638
Howard, David 369

Howard, James H. 17
Howard, Trevor 320
Hudson, Charles M. 18
Huffaker, Clair 353
Humberstone, H. Bruce 411
Hunt, Dennis 295
Huston, John 616
Hutton, Paul A. 119

IGNOBLE SAVAGE, THE: AMERICAN LITERARY RACISM, 1790-1890 2
IMAGE OF THE INDIAN AND THE BLACK MAN IN AMERICAN ART, 1590-1900, THE 30
Inca 189
Ince, Thomas H. 145
INCIDENT AT PHANTOM HILL 665
INDIAN FIGHTER, THE 530
INDIAN HISTORIAN, THE 1
INDIAN IN AMERICAN HISTORY, THE 49
INDIAN IN AMERICAN LITERATURE, THE 22
INDIAN KITSCH: THE USE AND MISUSE OF INDIAN IMAGES 36
INDIAN LIFE: TRANSFORMING AN AMERICAN MYTH 34
INDIAN LOVE CALL 375
INDIANS 107
INDIANS ARE COMING, THE 179
INDIAN UPRISING 470
Injun Joe 114, 131
INNOCENT EYE, THE: THE LIFE OF ROBERT J. FLAHERTY 77
INVASION OF AMERICA, THE: INDIANS, COLONIALISM AND THE CANT OF CONQUEST 19

Iocopi, Robert 14
IRON CAGES: RACE AND CULTURE IN NINETEENTH-CENTURY AMERICA 43
Iron Eyes Cody 176
IROQUOIS TRAIL, THE 433
ISHI IN TWO WORLDS 183

JACK MCCALL, DESPERADO 489
Jackson, Helen Hunt 7
Jackson, Martin A. 152
Jacobs, Tom 120
Jeavens, Clyde 296
Jennings, Francis 19
JEREMIAH JOHNSON 263, 300, 306, 337, 705
JIM THORPE--ALL AMERICAN 449
Johannsen, Albert 20
JOHNNY TIGER 666
Johnson, William 297
Jones, Daryl E. 121, 122
Jones, Harmon 546, 584
Jones, Ken D. 136
Josephy, Alvin M., Jr. 21
JOURNEY THROUGH ROSEBUD 256
Juran, Nathan 494, 506, 695

Kael, Pauline 298, 299, 300, 301
Kalem 210
KALEIDOSCOPIC LENS, THE: HOW HOLLYWOOD VIEWS ETHNIC GROUPS 66
Kaminsky, Stuart 302
Kane, Joseph 413, 453, 542
Karlson, Phil 433, 457, 518, 591

INDEX

Kasindorf, Martin 61
Katzin, Lee H. 690
Kaufman, Philip 709
Kaufmann, Donald L. 123
Kaufmann, Stanley 303, 304, 305, 306, 307, 308
Kay, Gilbert (Jose Briz) 689
Keams, Geraldine 120
Keighley, William 436
Keiser, Albert 22
Keller, Harry 571, 633
Kendall, Martha 124
Keneas, Alex 309
Kennedy, Burt 125, 619, 678
Kershner, Irvin 713
Keshena, Rita 126
KID RODELO 667
Kindem, Gorham 310
King, Henry 374
King, Louis 423, 424, 504, 554
KING OF THE WILD HORSES 404
KINGS OF THE SUN 639
KISS OF FIRE 531
KIT CARSON 387
Kitchin, Laurence 127
Kitses, Jim 128
Kjellin, Alf 698
Klain, S. 311
Knight, Arthur 312, 313, 314
Kopit, Arthur 107
Kramer, Frank (Gianfranco Parolini) 700
Kress, Howard F. 462
Kroll, Jack 315, 316

Lacey, Richard 129
LAND RAIDERS 695
Landers, Lew 431, 461, 480
Landres, Paul 569
Lang, Fritz 393
Lang, Richard 721
Larkins, Robert 130
LaRoque, Emma 23, 131
LAST FRONTIER, THE 532
LAST HUNT, THE 551
LAST OF THE COMANCHES 471
LAST OF THE MOHICANS, THE (1936) 112, 372
LAST OF THE MOHICANS, THE (1977) 715
LAST OF THE REDMEN 405
LAST OUTPOST, THE 450
LAST TRAIN FROM GUN HILL 601
LAST WAGON, THE 552
LATIN AMERICAN IMAGE IN AMERICAN FILM, THE 189
Laughlin, Frank (Tom) 708
Laughlin, Tom (T.C. Frank, Frank Laughlin) 132, 197, 703, 708
Laven, Arnold 630, 656
LAW AND JAKE WADE, THE 592
LeBorg, Reginald 442, 578
LEGEND OF THE LONE RANGER, THE 723
Lelchuk, Allen 317
LeRoy, Mervyn 512, 539, 600
Levin, Henry 519
Lewis, Joseph H. 561, 567
Lichtenstein, Grace 133, 134
LIGHT IN THE FOREST, THE 593
LITTLE BIG HORN 451

LITTLE BIG MAN 89, 109, 113, 118, 119, 151, 154, 155, 159, 215, 234, 240, 261, 266, 274, 299, 307, 323, 334, 354, 356, 362, 364, 696
Littlefeather, Sacheen 54
Livingston, Richard O. 135
Lloyd, Frank 378
Lockhart, Jane 318
Lone Ranger 124, 163
LONE RANGER, THE 112, 553
LONE RANGER AND THE LOST CITY OF GOLD, THE 594
LONE STAR 472
LOOK TO THE MOUNTAINTOP 14
Lopez, Andres 24
Lubin, Arthur 394
Lucas, Phil 120
LUST FOR GOLD 421
Lyman, Christopher M. 25
Lyon, Francis D. 599

McBride, Joseph 319, 320
McClure, Arthur F. 136
McCowan, George 699
McDonald, Frank 520
MCKENNA'S GOLD 691
McLaglen, Andrew V. 640, 679
McLeod, Norman 412, 597
MCLINTOCK 179, 640
MCMASTERS, THE 698
McNickle, D'Arcy 26
MacKenzie, Kent 623
MAJOR DUNDEE 128, 659
MAKING THE MOVIES 87

MAN CALLED HORSE, A 109, 155, 208, 226, 229, 244, 265, 269, 275, 276, 309, 313, 338, 357, 697
Manchell, Frank 137
MAN FROM LARAMIE, THE 533
MANITOU 237, 239, 251, 252, 716
Mann, Anthony 282, 432, 441, 464, 532, 533
Mann, Delbert 625
MAN'S FAVORITE SPORT? 649
Mantell, Harold 138
MANY RIVERS TO CROSS 534
Marin, Edwin L. 419, 429
Marsden, Michael T. 139
Marshall, George 396, 475, 556
Martinson, Leslie 637
Marton, Andrew 477
Maslin, Janet 321
MASSACRE (1934) 105, 151, 212, 370
MASSACRE (1956) 554
MASSACRE RIVER 422
Massai 284
MASS FOR THE DAKOTA SIOUX 85
MASTERSON OF KANSAS 509
Mate, Rudolph 514, 526, 632
May, Jill P. 140
Maynard, Richard A. 141
Merrill, Keith 718, 724
Metis, 23
Metoyer-Duran, Cheryl 142
Millar, Stuart 255, 707
Miller, Arthur 62, 720

INDEX

Miller, Don 143
Miller, Randall M. 66
Mills, Billy 279
Millstead, Thomas 144
Milne, Tom 322, 323, 324
Miner, Allen H. 573
Minority Casting Summary Report 162
MIRACLE RIDER, THE 112
MISSOURI BREAKS, THE 190
Mitchell, George 145
MOHAWK 555
Momaday, N. Scott 63
Monument Valley 71, 101, 125, 273
Moore, Michael 682
Morgan, Sir John 242, 248
Morgenstern, Joseph 146
Morris, Gary 325
Morse, Richardson 704
MOUNTAIN MEN, THE 721
MRS. MIKE 423
Mulligan, Richard 228
Mulligan, Robert 692
Murphey, A.D. 326, 327
Murphy, Sharon 27
MY DARLING CLEMENTINE 161, 402
MY LITTLE CHICKADEE 388

Nachbar, Jack (John) 139, 147, 148, 149, 155, 328
NANOOK OF THE NORTH 77, 91, 116, 332
Nash, Gary B. 28
National Film Committee of the Association of American Indian Affairs 138
Native Americans and Broadcasting 92
NATIVE AMERICANS ON FILM AND VIDEO 186
NATIVE SCHOOLING 153
Navajo 88, 94, 101, 177, 192
NAVAJO JOE 668
Nazarro, Ray 470, 500, 516, 564, 580
NEBRASKAN, THE 490
Nelson, Ralph 213, 329, 662, 701
Neumann, Kurt 409, 555
NEVADA SMITH 669
NEW ENGLAND FRONTIER: PURITANS AND INDIANS, 1620-1675 47
Newfeld, Sam 587
Newman, Joseph M. 474, 531, 589, 628
Newman, Paul 343
NEW MEXICO 452
Nichol, Dudley 247
NIGHTWING 720
Niver, Kent R. 150
NORTHWEST MOUNTED POLICE 216, 389
NORTHWEST OUTPOST 406
NORTHWEST PASSAGE 116, 203, 206, 217, 390
Noschese, Christine 29
NOW THAT THE BUFFALO ARE GONE 85

Oberbeck, S.K. 330
O'Connor, John E. 151, 152
OH! SUSANNA 453
OKLAHOMA TERRITORY 613
OKLAHOMAN, THE 568
Oman, Mary M. 153
ONE FLEW OVER THE CUCKOO'S NEST 61,

ONE FLEW OVER THE
  CUCKOO'S NEST (cont'd)
  133, 710
ONE REEL A WEEK 62
ONLY GOOD INDIAN. . .,
  THE: THE HOLLYWOOD
  GOSPEL 107, 108, 158
ONLY THE VALIANT 454
OREGON PASSAGE 569
OREGON TRAIL, THE 602
Oulahan, Richard 331
OUTLAW JOSEY WALES, THE
  712
OUTRIDERS, THE 434
OUTSIDER, THE 129, 159,
  625
OVERLAND PACIFIC 510

PAGANS IN OUR MIDST 24
PALEFACE, THE 412
Parolini, Gianfranco
  (Frank Kramer) 700
Parry, Ellwood 30
PATHFINDER, THE 473
Patterson, F.T. 332
Pauly, Thomas H. 154
PAWNEE 570
Pawnee Bill 32
Pearce, Roy Harvey 31
Pechter, William S. 333,
  334
Peckinpah, Sam 128, 622,
  659
Penn, Arthur 89, 228,
  240, 261, 266, 299,
  334, 356, 362, 364, 696
Perkins, V. F. 335
Pevney, Joseph 528, 614
Philipps, Harold 671
PICTORIAL HISTORY OF THE
  WESTERN FILM, A 96
Pierce, Charles B. 714,
  726

Pilkington, William T.
  155
PILLARS OF THE SKY 556
Pink, Sidney 655, 673
Place, J.A. 156
PLAINSMAN, THE (1936)
  218, 373
PLAINSMAN, THE (1966)
  670
PLUNDERERS, THE (1948)
  413
PLUNDERERS, THE (1960)
  614
Polonsky, Abraham 146,
  204, 324, 693
Pollack, Sydney 685,
  705
PONY EXPRESS 491
PONY SOLDIER 474
POSSE FROM HELL 626
Preminger, Otto 511
PRETEND INDIANS, THE:
  IMAGES OF NATIVE
  AMERICANS IN THE
  MOVIES 67
Price, John A. 157
PROUD AND THE PROFANE,
  THE 557
Public Broadcasting and
  Native Americans 92
PURPLE HILLS, THE 627

QUANTEZ 571

RACE RELATIONS IN BRITISH
  NORTH AMERICA, 1607-
  1783 16
RACHEL AND THE STRANGER
  414
Rader, Dotson 336
Rafkin, Alan 686
RAIDERS, THE 641
RAINBOW TRAIL, THE 366

RAMONA 219, 259, 374
RAMPAGE AT APACHE WELLS 671
Rarihokwats 158
RAWHIDE TRAIL, THE 595
Rawlins, John 422, 448
Ray, Nicholas 604
Redford, Robert 120, 300, 306
RED MAN IN ART, THE 9
RED MOUNTAIN 455
RED RIVER 415
RED TOMAHAWK 677
RED, WHITE AND BLACK: THE PEOPLES OF EARLY AMERICA 28
RED, WHITE, AND BLACK: SYMPOSIUM ON INDIANS IN THE OLD SOUTH 18
Reed, Carol 694
REGENERATION THROUGH VIOLENCE: THE MYTHOLOGY OF THE AMERICAN FRONTIER, 1600-1860 40
Reinl, Harold 653, 660
Reis, Irving 452
REPRISAL 558
RETURN OF A MAN CALLED HORSE, THE 134, 242, 248, 250, 258, 262, 270, 276, 296, 713
REVOLT AT FORT LARAMIE 572
Reynolds, Lynn 366
Rice, Susan 159
Rich, David Lowell 670
Richburg, James R. 160
RIDE BACK, THE 573
RIDE 'EM COWBOY 394
RIDE LONESOME 603
RIDE OUT FOR REVENGE 574
Riesner, Charles F. 438

Rieupeyrout, Jean-Louis 161
RIO CONCHOS 650
RIO GRANDE 435
Ritt, Martin 676
RIVER OF NO RETURN 511
Robb, David 162
ROCKY MOUNTAIN 436
Roger's Rangers 206
Ronan, Margaret 337, 338
ROSE MARIE (1936) 375
ROSE MARIE (1954) 512
Rosenbaum, Jonathan 339, 340
Rothel, David 163
Rothwell, Stephen J. 164
Rouse, Russell 606
Rousseau, Jean Jacques 3
Rowland, Roy 165, 434, 467, 534
Rudolph, Oscar 635
RUNNING BRAVE 279, 727
RUN OF THE ARROW 179, 225, 575
RUN, SIMON, RUN 699
Rush, Richard 684
Russell, Don 32

SABATA 700
SACRED GROUND 726
Sale, Richard 437
Salkow, Sidney 473, 489, 515, 644, 657
Salzman, Bert 111
Sampson, Will 61, 133
San Carlos Indian 355
SAND 424
Sando, Joe S. 33
SANTE FE PASSAGE 535
Sarris, Andrew 341

SASKATCHEWAN 513
SAVAGE, THE 475
Savage, William W., Jr. 34
SAVAGE INNOCENTS, THE 220, 604
SAVAGE SAM 642
SAVAGE SEVEN, THE 684
SAVAGES OF AMERICA, THE: A STUDY OF THE INDIAN AND THE IDEA OF CIVILIZATION 31
SAVAGISM AND CIVILITY: INDIANS AND ENGLISHMEN IN COLONIAL VIRGINIA 167
SAVAGISM AND CIVILIZATION: A STUDY OF THE INDIAN AND THE AMERICAN MIND 31
SCALPHUNTERS, THE 685
Scheick, William J. 35
Scheuer, Philip K. 342
Schickel, Richard 343, 344, 345
Schmitz, Tony 166
Scholder, Fritz 36
Schuster, Harold 566
Schwartz, Joseph 37
Screen Actors' Guild 162
SEARCHERS, THE 71, 287, 294, 310, 319, 325, 351, 559
Sears, Fred F. 478, 490, 510, 522, 581
Seaton, George 557
SECRET OF TREASURE MOUNTAIN, THE 560
Seiter, William 380, 384
Seitz, George B. 372, 387

Selander, Lesley 445, 468, 486, 496, 498, 521, 527, 538, 572, 594, 683
Sell, Henry B. 38
SEMINOLE 492
SEMINOLE UPRISING 536
SERGEANT RUTLEDGE 615
SERGEANTS 3 631
Serving Native American Media Needs 92
SEVEN CITIES OF GOLD 537
SEVEN SEAS TO CALAIS 632
SEVENTH CAVALRY 561
SHADOWS OF THE INDIAN: STEREOTYPES IN AMERICAN CULTURE 42
SHAKIEST GUN IN THE WEST, THE 686
SHALAKO 687
Shales, Tom 346
Sharp, Alan 278
Shaughnessy, Tim 39
Sheperd, Duncan 347
Sher, Jack 607
SHERIFF OF FRACTURED JAW, THE 605
Sherman, Vincent 472
SHE WORE A YELLOW RIBBON 179, 191, 425
Sholem, Lee 493
SHOOT OUT AT MEDICINE BEND 576
Shoshone 174
SHOTGUN 538
Sidney, George 427
SIEGE AT RED RIVER 514
Siegel, Don 611
Silet, Charles L.P. 64, 65, 66, 67, 167, 168, 169

Silverheels, Jay 98
SILVER RIVER 416
Silverstein, Elliott 208, 276, 313, 654, 697
Simon, J. 348
Simon, S. Sylvan 398, 421
Sinclair, Andrew 170
Siodmak, Robert 680
Sioux 144, 145, 226, 244, 275, 309
Sirk, Douglas 517
Sitting Bull 98, 230, 257, 272, 333
SITTING BULL 515
SIX BLACK HORSES 633
SIX-GUN MYSTIQUE, THE 82
SIX GUNS AND SOCIETY 190, 193
SLAUGHTER TRAIL 456
Sloane, Paul H. 382
Slotkin, Richard 40
Smith, Alan M. 16
Smith, Captain John 7
Smith, James R. 171
Smith, Robert C. 41
SOLDIER BLUE 109, 159, 205, 213, 236, 277, 281, 329, 330, 336, 358, 360, 701
SON OF PALEFACE, THE 476
SOUTHWEST PASSAGE 516
Spears, Jack 172, 173
Spenser, Richard V. 174
Springsteen, R.G. 645, 648, 652, 661, 677
SQUAW MAN, THE 179, 367
Stabiner, Karen 175, 349
STAGECOACH (1939) 101, 233, 247, 383
STAGECOACH (1966) 672
STAGECOACH TO DANCER'S ROCK 634
STAGE TO THUNDER ROCK 651
STALKING MOON, THE 692
Stanbrook, Alan 350
STAND AT APACHE RIVER 493
STAY AWAY, JOE 688
Stedman, Raymond William 42
Steiner, Stan 176
Steinman, Clay 351
Stevens, George 371
Stewart, Jimmy 342
STRANGE LADY IN TOWN 539
STREETS OF LAREDO 457
Sturges, John 484, 545, 592, 601, 631, 658
Sufrin, Mark 352
Sun Valley Western Film Conference 97
SUSANNAH OF THE MOUNTIES 384

TAGGART 652
TAHTONKA 183
TAILFEATHERS 153
Takaki, Ronald T. 43
Talbot, Anne 177
TALL MEN, THE 540
TALL WOMEN, THE 673
Tashlin, Frank 476
Taurog, Norman 618
Taylor, Don 702
TAZA, SON OF COCHISE 517
TELL THEM WILLIE BOY IS HERE 86, 109, 146, 151, 159, 204, 295,

TELL THEM WILLIE BOY IS
  HERE (cont'd) 298, 324,
  344, 693
TEN GENTLEMEN FROM WEST
  POINT 395
Tenkate, Herman F.C. 44
Terraine, John 178
TEXAS ACROSS THE RIVER
  674
TEXAS RANGERS, THE 376
TEXTBOOKS AND THE AMERICAN
  INDIAN 10
THERE MUST BE A LONE
  RANGER 76
THESE ARE MY PEOPLE 241
THEY DIED WITH THEIR
  BOOTS ON 151, 214, 221,
  288, 359, 392
THEY RODE WEST 518
THOMAS NAST: POLITICAL
  CARTOONIST 48
Thompson, Howard 353
Thompson, J. Lee 639
  691, 717
Thorpe, Jerry 681
THREE REPORTS ON SERVING
  NATIVE AMERICAN BROAD-
  CAST NEEDS 92
THREE WARRIORS 718
THREE YOUNG TEXANS 519
THROUGH NAVAJO EYES: AN
  EXPLORATION IN FILM
  COMMUNICATION AND
  ANTHROPOLOGY 192
THUNDER IN THE SUN 606
THUNDER OF DRUMS, A
  628
THUNDER PASS 520
TICKET TO TOMAHAWK, A
  437
Tokar, Norman 642
TOMAHAWK 458
Tom Black Bull 245

TOM SAWYER 114, 131
TONKA 596
Tonto 124
Tourneur, Jacques 400,
  550
TRAVELING SALESWOMAN,
  THE 438
TREASURE OF SILVER LAKE,
  THE 660
Trenner, Robert A. 45
TRIAL OF BILLY JACK 260,
  708
TRIUMPHS OF A MAN CALLED
  HORSE III 725
TROOPER HOOK 577
TULSA 426
TUMBLEWEED 494
Turner, John 155, 354
Tuska, Jon 179
Twain, Mark 114
Tweksbury, Peter 688
TWINKLE IN GOD'S EYES,
  THE 541
TWO FLAGS WEST 439
TWO RODE TOGETHER 129,
  629

ULZANA'S RAID 113, 155
  243, 253, 278, 302, 328,
  345, 347, 706
UNCONQUERED 407
UNFORGIVEN, THE 616
UNION PACIFIC 385
U.S. Commission on Civil
  Rights 180, 181
Ute 255

VALLEY OF THE SUN 396
Van Der Beets, Richard
  46
Van Dyke II, W.S. 375
VANISHING AMERICAN, THE
  151, 280, 346, 542

INDEX

VANISHING RACE AND OTHER ILLUSIONS, THE: PHOTOGRAPHS OF INDIANS BY EDWARD S. CURTIS 25
Vaughan, Alden T. 47
Vestal, Stanley 182
Vickrey, William 183
Vidor, King 376, 390, 401
Vinson, J. Chal 48
Vogel, Virgil 49
Vohrer, Alfred 664

Wagenknecht, Edward 184
Waggner, George 570
WAGON MASTER 440
Walbridge, Earl F. 355
Walker, Beverly 132
Walker, Stanley 185
WALK TALL 617
WALK THE PROUD LAND 222, 289, 352, 355, 562
Walsh, Moria 356, 357, 358
Walsh, Raoul 359, 365, 392, 416, 420, 446, 513, 523, 540, 605, 647
WAR ARROW 495
WAR DRUMS 578
Warner Brothers 197, 335
WARPATH 459
WAR PAINT 496
Warren, Charles Marquis 451, 479, 577, 582
WAR, THE WEST, AND THE WILDERNESS, THE 74
WAR WAGON, THE 678
Wayne, John 287, 294, 325
WAY OUT WEST 377
WAY WEST, THE 679

Weatherford, Elizabeth 186
Webb, Robert D. 537, 543
Weber, Alexander 93
Weidman, Bette S. 7
Wellman, William 397, 417, 443, 460
WELLS FARGO 378
Wendkos, Paul 666
Westerbeck, Colin L., Jr. 360, 361
WESTERN, THE: AN ILLUSTRATED GUIDE 98
WESTERN, THE: FROM SILENTS TO THE SEVENTIES 100
WESTERN FILMS: AN ANNOTATED CRITICAL BIBLIOGRAPHY 149
WESTERN FILMS OF JOHN FORD, THE 156
WESTERN MOVIES 155, 328
WESTERNS 106
WESTERNS: ASPECTS OF A MOVIE GENRE 105
WESTERN UNION 393
WESTWARD HO THE WAGONS! 563
WESTWARD THE WOMEN 460
Weyright, Victor 38
Whelan, Tim 399
WHEN THE LEGENDS DIE 113, 223, 245, 255, 707
WHEN THE REDSKINS RODE 461
WHITE BUFFALO, THE 224, 717
WHITE COMANCHE 689
WHITE DAWN, THE 118, 709
WHITE FEATHER 543
WHITE MAN'S INDIAN, THE

WHITE MAN'S INDIAN, THE (cont'd) 6
WHITE ON RED: IMAGES OF THE AMERICAN INDIAN 7
White River Reservation 342
WHITE SQUAW, THE 564
WHO WAS THAT MASKED MAN? THE STORY OF THE LONE RANGER 163
WILD AND THE INNOCENT, THE 607
WILD NORTH, THE 477
WILD WEST, THE: A HISTORY OF THE WILD WEST SHOWS 32
WILD WESTERNERS, THE 635
Wild West Show 37, 38
WILD WOMEN 702
Wilkinson, Gerald 187
Willett, Ralph 188
Williams, Elmo 565
WILL JAMES' SAND 424
Wilmington, Michael 319
Wilson, Charles Reagan 50
WINCHESTER '73 441
WINDOW DRESSING ON THE SET: AN UPDATE 181
WINDOW DRESSING ON THE SET: WOMEN AND MINORITIES IN TELEVISION 180
WINDWALKER 118, 254, 320, 321, 724
WINTERHAWK 246, 714
Wise, Robert 408, 439
Witney, William 379, 535, 643, 663
Woll, Allen 189
Wood, Michael 190
Wood, Robin 191, 362
Wood, Sam 418

WORLDS BETWEEN TWO RIVERS, THE: PERSPECTIVES ON AMERICAN INDIANS IN IOWA 168
Worth, Sol 192
Wounded Knee 27
Wright, Will 190, 193

Yacowar, Maurice 194, 363
YELLOW SKY 417
YELLOWSTONE KELLY 608
YELLOW TOMAHAWK 521
YOU ARE ON INDIAN LAND 111, 241
YOUNG DANIEL BOONE 442
YOUNG GUNS OF TEXAS 636
Youngson, Robert 621

Zimmerman, Paul D. 364

**WITHDRAWN FROM
THE ELLEN CLARKE BERTRAND LIBRARY**